BEHAVIOR MODIFICATION WITH CHILDREN

BEHAVIOR MODIFICATION WITH CHILDREN

A Clinical Training Manual

By

ALEXANDER J. TYMCHUK, Ph.D.

University of California
Los Angeles, California

CHARLES C THOMAS • PUBLISHER
Springfield • Illinois • U.S.A.

Published and Distributed Throughout the World by
CHARLES C THOMAS • PUBLISHER
Bannerstone House
301-327 East Lawrence Avenue, Springfield, Illinois, U.S.A.

With THOMAS BOOKS *careful attention is given to all details of manufacturing and design. It is the Publisher's desire to present books that are satisfactory as to their physical qualities and artistic possibilities and appropriate for their particular use.* THOMAS BOOKS *will be true to those laws of quality that assure a good name and good will.*

Printed in the United States of America
N-10

Library of Congress Cataloging in Publication Data

Tymchuk, Alexander J
    Behavior modification with children.

    Bibliography: p.
    1. Behavior therapy. 2. Child psychiatry.
I. Title. [DNLM: 1. Behavior therapy — In infancy and childhood.
WM420 T986b 1974]
RJ505.B4T95   618.9'28'914   74-715
ISBN 0-398-03124-X
ISBN 0-398-03125-8 (pbk.)

PREFACE

THIS BOOK IS MEANT to serve as a manual for training people in the clinical aspects of behavior modification with children and can be used in conjunction with a book on the theory of operant conditioning. Ellen Reese's *The Analysis of Human Operant Behavior* (Dubuque, Iowa, Wm. C. Brown, 1966) is very suitable for this purpose. The manual should be used in a class, a laboratory or a group setting where practice with the techniques and observation of models can be done to supplement the contents of the book. In order that each person knows the techniques well, each can monitor and manipulate a single behavior of their own. Or they can practice the techniques on one of their peers. The techniques can be part of the practical exercises for the course and can be adapted to suit the occasion, that is, whether in the special class or on the ward or in the laboratory or in the home. A useful strategy is to cover only one chapter at a time so that the students do not begin prematurely to attempt to manipulate behavior in their target subject.

This manual has largely been used in training on an individual basis as part of an internship experience. Undergraduate students have been effectively taught to use behavior modification techniques first in a group setting with observation and later by actual application of the techniques. Parents have been taught, both individually and in groups, to eliminate maladaptive behaviors and to shape appropriate behaviors in their children. These are parents who are having extreme difficulties in handling their child's behavior. The children include those who have been diagnosed as psychotic or autistic or as mentally retarded and behavior problematic. In all cases the parents have demonstrated that they can become effective trainers through the use of behavior modification techniques. Parents have also demonstrated that they can generalize their training to other aspects of life with their child and even apply these techniques with siblings of the target child.

Graphing is not always necessary later in training, but often parents will continue to graph because they find the visible results of their progress reinforcing.

Articles describing the parent and student training programs are available. These programs include instructions on how to run a parent training group. There is also a description of a walkie-talkie device for communicating with the trainer while he is working with the child and information on the use of videotaping. There are additional descriptions of programs to develop self-play, receptive and expressive language, social interaction of autistic children with their peers, and to develop self-help and preacademic skills in autistic and retarded children. These articles are all available on request to the author, and the author would appreciate comments on the programs and the present manual.

Finally, as in any other programs, consistency must be stressed. Trainees must be trained to be consistent in their application of behavior modification techniques. Two words of caution to the trainers: increasingly, behavior modification techniques are being disseminated to disparate groups of people as part of short workshop experiences, thus not allowing those trained to be thoroughly versed in the correct application of the techniques and not allowing the trainers to supervise that application. As trainers, we must be careful in this regard since we are dealing with very potent training techniques which if used correctly can be extremely useful with a variety of populations as research has shown; however, if the techniques are used incorrectly despite the trainer's intentions, a great deal of harm can ensue. We must monitor, at least for a time, those whom we train to use these techniques.

Secondly, we must not lose sight of the fact that behavior modification is a group of techniques, a technology, and does not constitute an educational program. We must not reify behavior modification for itself; its effectiveness comes from applying the methodology to other content areas such as academic skills. Thus, parents and others trained in the usage of the technology should be taught its limitations as well; the technology tells us how to teach, but not what to teach. The what must come from a rapprochement of several areas of research and from an extension of the current behavior modification model.

ACKNOWLEDGMENTS

THE AUTHOR WOULD LIKE to acknowledge the help of Rayna Rudominer, M.A., in the writing of an earlier draft of this manuscript as well as in working with some of the cases used as examples in this book; the help of Carol Horowitz, Ph.D., Steven Lorber, M.A., Darrell Burnett, Ph.D., James Q. Simmons, III, M.D., Alan Insul and Danielle Berger, as well as the many parents, particularly Connie and Harvey Lapin, and the many undergraduate students who were involved in training or being trained and who made invaluable comments on this book in its formative stages; the support of his wife, Pauline, and the help of his secretary, Tobi Hernandez; and finally Robert Alvarez of the UCLA Mental Retardation Media Group for his graphic work. The author's work is supported in part by Maternal and Child Health Grant #927.

CONTENTS

BEHAVIOR MODIFICATION WITH CHILDREN

CHAPTER I

INTRODUCTION

THE ORIGINS of some of the principles of behavior modification extend to the times of the Greeks, but that which we now know as behavior modification had its beginnings with Thorndike, an American psychologist.

THORNDIKE

In the early 1900's, Thorndike, in working with animals, studied ways to improve their ability to discriminate and to learn simple mazes. As a result of these studies, he stated his Law of Effect in which he said:

> Of several responses made to the same situation, those which are accompanied or closely followed by satisfaction to the animal will . . . be more firmly connected with the situation, so that, when it recurs, they will become likely to recur; those which are accompanied or closely followed by discomfort to the animal will . . . have their connections with that situation weakened, so that, when it recurs, they will be less likely to recur. The greater the satisfaction or discomfort, the greater the strengthening or weakening of the bond (Thorndike, 1911).

This statement is the predecessor of the use of reinforcement. Thorndike did not apply his ideas only to animals; he also applied them to the teaching situation, where he felt that the effective teacher should identify the bonds to be formed or broken, the states of affairs which should satisfy or annoy, and the means to apply the satisfaction and annoyances (Thorndike, 1913).

SKINNER'S OPERANT CONDITIONING

Thorndike's ideas were elaborated upon and restated by B.F. Skinner, a psychologist at Harvard. His work, too, began with identifying the laws that governed learning in animals. Skinner, like Thorndike, chose to work with animals because they were readily available to practice with when ideas were being tested. Skinner also applied his ideas to the education of people, especially through the use of programmed instruction. Programmed instruction is an instructional device in which materials to be learned are organized in a systematic fashion for presentation by a machine.

Skinner found that learning in animals followed definite rules, that aberrant behavior could be instituted in animals, and that these behaviors could be extinguished.

It was left up to other researchers to demonstrate that many of the rules of learning with animals also applied to humans. Other researchers began applying these principles to the weakening and extinguishing of maladaptive behaviors, as well as the shaping of more adaptive behaviors in adults and children. Since these earlier studies, the principles of behavior modification have been applied with retarded or otherwise developmentally disabled children in training them to use the toilet properly; to dress, clean and feed themselves; and to speak, read and make visual discriminations, as well as to learn other academic skills. The principles of behavior modification have been used to stop maladaptive behaviors in these children such as head-banging, biting themselves, temper tantrums, hyperactivity, aggressiveness, and excessive crying. These principles have also been applied to increase social interaction between these children and their peers.

A "Vegetative Idiot" Moves[1]

An early example of the application of Skinner's techniques to humans was done with a young man who was institutionalized and diagnosed as a "vegetative idiot"! Many of these types of cases can be seen on back wards of some institutions for the retarded. These people may be young or old, but they just lie there in their cribs, being fed, being cleaned, immobile except for an eyeblink or defecation; they just exist. The aides, in the meantime, have to

---

[1]Fuller, P.: Operant conditioning of a vegetative human organism. *Am J Psychol,* *62*:587-590, 1949.

perform all things for them.

The implication is, of course, that these people are incapable of any willful behavior. In the above case it was noted that this young man occasionally moved his right arm while lying there. It was further observed that when the aides fed him, they only did so when he was still thus reinforcing stationary behavior *for a person whom they complained never moved.* For a first session, the experimenters observed the number of times the man raised his arm each minute to get a baseline. In the next three sessions they gave him a syringe full of warm, sugar-milk solution each time he raised his arm. As a result, the man raised his arm to a vertical position from once each minute on the first day, to three times each minute on the fourth. The man could move purposefully.

To prove that their manipulation had been the critical factor, the experimenters stopped giving the man the milk and his arm raising extinguished completely.

This case is important because it demonstrated that even one of the worst cases on a back ward could be trained to do a simple motion. Although the experimenters stopped there, they felt that the young man could have been trained to do more. It may be that he could then have been trained to reach a bar over his head, to clasp it, to apply pressure, to lift himself up a little, and more and more each day, to clasp a spoon, to bring it to his mouth and so on. The importance of this example also lies in the fact that something can be done, and it demonstrates that one principle of learning (that positive reinforcement increases the probability of a response) which had been seen with animals, also works with humans.

Training Mute Autistic Children to Speak[2,3]

Most people know that autistic children do not speak and are very limited behaviorally. Yet some autistic children have been

---

[2]Kerr, N., Meyerson, L., and Michael, J.: A procedure for shaping vocalizations in a mute child. In Ullman, L., and Krasner, L.: *Case Studies in Behavior Modification.* New York, H. R. & W, 1965.

[3]Lovaas, O.: *Teaching Language to Psychotic Children* (a film). New York, Appleton, 1969.

trained to do simple tasks in order to get candy instead of just sitting and rocking and have been trained to say words when previously they made no sound whatsoever. What is so phenomenal about this?

This is phenomenal because, in the past, people considered that autistic children were not able to do anything; therefore the child was to be considered a burden for the duration of his life. This is also phenomenal because parents of autistic children can experience even the tiniest ray of hope and feel some sense of competence and fulfillment.

Jane was a mute, three-year-old girl who did not walk, talk, laugh, cry or interact with others. She broke things. Jane was brought in and placed on the experimenter's knees. Each time she made a noise, she was cuddled and jiggled and given a candy. After six 20-minute sessions, Jane went from making no vocalizations to making seven clear vocalizations. Then the experimenter only gave her a candy each time she made a vocalization immediately after his vocalization. After an initial drop in vocal output, the child responded consistently after the experimenter.

Another case was Ricky, who did not look at anyone or did not speak. He was five years old and considered to be psychotic. He was encouraged to follow the instructions "Look at me." This was started when each time that he accidentally looked at the experimenter, he would be given a spoon of ice cream. Gradually the pairing of the verbal command with the ice cream was such that Ricky looked at the experimenter each time the command was given. The next step, then, became to get Ricky to emit a sound. Each time Ricky made a sound, he was given ice cream. Once he made the sound reliably, the experimenter began having Ricky look at his lips when he said "ball." In this way Ricky came to say "b-b-b," "b," "ba," "ba-ba," and finally "ball." Ricky then learned to imitate several other words relatively easily. These two latter programs are practical examples of shaping.

Eliminating Temper Tantrums[4]

Another principle of operant conditioning is that of extinction. Charles was twenty-one months old and had been seriously ill for much of his life, but was now improving so that he had gained weight and appeared normal. However, Charles continued to demand the same special care and attention as he had previously received, especially at bedtime when he would scream and fuss if the parent left the room before he fell asleep. If the parent read in the bedroom while waiting for him to fall asleep, Charles would cry until the parent stopped reading. The time spent in settling him to sleep was often as much as two hours.

As a strategy, the parents were instructed to put Charles to bed in a friendly, relaxed manner and to leave, closing the door after them and not returning. The child screamed and cried for forty-five minutes the first night, but did not cry at all the second night; he cried for ten minutes the third night, but by the eighth night he had stopped completely and even smiled when put to bed. A week later, however, Charles again cried at bedtime. On this occasion an aunt was babysitting; she came in to see what was wrong and thus inadvertently reinforced crying again. The program had to start over again but was equally successful.

Each of the above practical examples of Skinner's operant principles were early pioneering efforts and demonstrated clearly that these techniques could be used in the weakening of maladaptive behaviors as in the cases of Ricky and Jane. These cases were individual ones with only a few people involved; later we will discuss similar programs applied to groups of children.

PAVLOV'S CLASSICAL CONDITIONING

Another avenue of behavior modification research derives from Pavlov's work. In the early 1900's in Russia, Pavlov found that repeatedly pairing a bell with the sight of food made a hungry dog salivate. Soon just presenting the bell without food elicited salivation in the dog. This type of conditioning was termed

---

[4]Williams, C.: The elimination of tantrum behavior by extinction procedures. *J Abnorm Psychol, 58:*269, 1959.

classical conditioning, distinguishing it from the operant conditioning of Skinner. It is important to notice one difference in the types of conditioning. In the classical or Pavlovin type, the organism's response is very automatic, or reflexive, and the environment acts on the organism to elicit the response. In the operant, or Skinnerian, type of conditioning the organism's behavior is purposeful in acting on the environment; the organism's behavior is then brought under the control of its consequences. For example, a boy who chooses a red block in response to the verbal command "pick up the red block," will receive verbal praise and will be more likely to pick up the red block the next time as well.

Although most behavior modification as applied to the mentally retarded is derived from Skinner's work, the extensions of Pavlov's work have had some applicability in the treatment of abnormal fears (phobias), tics, enuresis (bladder problem), encopresis (bowel problem), sexual disorders, and alcoholism. Much of this work has been done primarily with adults, but some has been done with children.

WATSON

Watson, an American psychologist, in the 1920's extended some of Pavlov's ideas to show that some abnormal fears are learned and can be unlearned. In a now classic case, Watson and his colleague Rosalie Rayner demonstrated how an eleven-month-old child, Albert, acquired a fear. These authors first presented Albert with burning newspapers; masks with and without hair; and a dog, rabbit, monkey and white rat. Little Albert did not display any fear reaction to any of these; however, when a loud noise (striking a hammer against a steel bar) was presented:

> The child started violently, his breathing was checked and the arms were raised in a characteristic manner. On the second stimulation the same thing occurred, and in addition the lips began to pucker and tremble. On the third stimulation, the child broke into a sudden crying fit.[5]

---

[5]Watson, J., and Rayner, R.: Conditioned emotional reactions. *J Exp Psychol, 3:* 1-14, 1920.

The authors then presented the rat along with the noise and the child jumped away from the rat, but did not cry. The next time Albert whimpered. There then followed a week of no presentations and then five more presentations: The instant the rat was shown the baby began to cry (pg.5). The baby was "afraid" of the rat only. Unfortunately, Albert was removed from the hospital before his conditioned reaction could be extinguished. In Jones' case,[6] Peter, a two-year-old boy, disliked to have rabbits near him. Over a period of days during which a rabbit in a cage was brought closer as Peter ate candy, Peter became less and less wary of the rabbit, so that he could ultimately play with the rabbit.

Elimination of School Phobias

Perhaps a more practical example of how fears develop and can be extinguished in children is in the case of school phobia. A child may be too attached to his mother and may not want to leave her. For this child, the school may be threatening. Jimmy[7], a boy of ten, had an intense fear of losing his mother. This fear had been initiated by the mother and paired with the school. The mother had repeatedly told Jimmy that someday she would be dead and that one day, after school, she would be gone. The school, previously neutral, came to elicit the fear reaction; Jimmy did not want to leave his mother for fear of her not being there when he returned. The mother further reinforced his avoiding school by keeping him at home.

The strategy in stopping this fear was to take Jimmy in the car to the school, where he and the psychologist sat and systematically moved up the walk, up the steps, down the hall, to the room, into the room with the teacher, in the room with two classmates and finally, with all the classmates present over a period of twenty days. Jimmy's fear has not returned after two years. Of course, the mother had to be told not to continue her statements.

---

[6]Jones, M.: The elimination of childrens' fears. *J Exp Psychol*, 7:382-390, 1924.

[7]Garvey, W., and Hegrenes, S.: Desensitization techniques in the treatment of school phobia. *Am J Orthopsychiatry, 36:*147-152, 1966.

Elimination of a Dog Phobia

There are numerous other examples of how a child develops fears, especially of dogs (after being bitten), of elevators, and of falling. In a recent case a young retarded boy with an extreme fear of dogs and other animals was seen. It was presumed that he had been bitten by the dog at home; however, it was found that both parents cared more for the dog than for the boy. The parents reportedly yelled at the boy when he was playing with the dog and said that even the dog was better behaved than he was. The child came to associate the dog and all animals with a fear or retribution.

The method chosen to correct this fear was to systematically socially interact with him and to give him food while bringing pictures of animals, toys, a live rabbit, a guinea pig, and finally a dog into the room with him.

Initially, the animals were in cages and covered in a corner, then uncovered and brought closer, and then released and played with by the boy. The parents were also cautioned about their statements.

These examples of applications of classical conditioning show that these techniques are efficacious with some maladaptive behaviors when used properly. The technique of pairing a pleasant stimulus while bringing closer a feared object or bringing the child closer to the feared object is also called systematic desensitization, which is its technical name. Systematic desensitization is often used in allaying the fears of retarded children to the dentist's drill, to fear of a new situation or place, to fear of a new teacher. This technique, however, is limited in its applicability because it emphasizes the removal of an abnormal behavior without an equal emphasis upon building more adaptive behaviors.

However, Skinner's operant conditioning is particularly useful for both removing maladaptive behaviors and building adaptive behaviors. For this reason operant conditioning, or behavior modification, has been used more with the retarded or developmentally disabled.

This book will stress operant methods and how they can be applied in the home by parents, in the school by teachers, on the ward by aides, and by professors responsible for training both graduate and undergraduate students in the clinical application of behavior modification with children.

CHAPTER II

THE TECHNOLOGY

DEFINING, COUNTING AND GRAPHING

In the previous section there was an introduction to the history of some of the concepts of behavior modification, as well as some examples of how these concepts have been applied. The examples were by way of introduction; a basic part of each example was the establishing of what it is that must be changed (e.g. temper tantrums), what this target behavior is exactly (e.g. crying when put to bed), and how often and when it occurs (e.g. every night at bedtime). This systematic analysis is also a part of behavior modification, as is systematic record keeping.

Defining The Problem Behavior

When most parents seek help with their child they state the problem rather loosely, saying that he is sloppy, immature, or aggressive. Each of these terms is vague and, as such, open to interpretation by the child, the parent, or anyone else. Being sloppy for one child may mean leaving clothes on the bed or never combing his hair for another, or not tying his shoes for another. Being immature may be crying or whining for no reason for one child, or hanging onto his mother for another, or not feeding or dressing himself for another. Being aggressive may be swearing for one child, or pushing for another, or actual hitting for a third child.

It is important to know exactly what the problem is for a particular child. This behavior then becomes the focal point of an intervention program.

Defining The Adaptive Behavior

It is always good to define exactly what it is you expect the child to do. Usually "good" behavior can be defined in terms of the opposite to the bad behavior. The opposite of sloppy is neat and of immature is mature, but again these are vague terms. Neat should be defined exactly, as hair combed, face washed, hands washed and dried, nails clean, shirt buttoned, and so on. Often to facilitate knowing what must be done and what is expected, both for the trainer and for the child, a list can be made and kept. Table I has an example.

TABLE I.
DEFINING "BEING NEAT"

Major Command	*Secondary Segments*	*Tertiary Segments*
	Dress yourself	Put on shirt
		Button shirt
		Put on pants
		Button pants
		Put on shoes
		Tie shoelaces
Be Neat		
	Wash yourself	Wash face
		Wash hands
		Dry face
		Dry hands
		Shower
	Toiletting	Clean fingernails
		Brush teeth
		Comb hair

Making a list of the good behaviors forces you to look critically at what a child does, and it may be seen that too much is expected of him or that he in fact does things for which he is not credited. For example, he may be able to put on his shirt, but may be unable to button it. Seeing him with his shirt unbuttoned may convey the impression of his being sloppy. But it may be that his fine motor movements may be limited, or he may be just too young to do this task. *Caution:* Before demands are made of a child, make sure acts required are within the child's normal developmental abilities. If the child is slower developmentally, this too should be considered. Many parents who do not have the experience of seeing little children in action may consider their child to be too noisy or to run too much or to cry too much. Each of these is normal for younger children, so that no emphasis need be placed on remedying so-called "deviant" behavior.

Too often parents focus on that which a child *cannot* do and virtually ignore all the things a child *can* do. The feeling is that good behavior will take care of itself. This is not true! If a child does something well and another thing poorly, but only gets criticized for the poorly done thing while the well-done thing is ignored, the child may cease doing the good thing. The parent virtually extinguishes the child's good behavior. By taking a close look at what a child does in fact do when a program is set up, the child can be reinforced for the things he does well, too, thereby giving him successful experiences.

Counting Behaviors—Frequency

All pinpointed or target behaviors must be countable. That is, each behavior must be defined so that an objective measure of the strength and magnitude of the behavior can be made. You must be able to count the *frequency* of the behavior, that is, the number of times the behavior occurs during a given time period. Examples of counting are (1) the number of temper tantrums each afternoon or each hour; (2) the number of times the brother is hit during meals; (3) the number of times the bed is made each week; (4) the number of times toys are asked for in an hour. It is quite a simple thing to count the frequency of a given behavior, and yet many parents will not take the time to do so. These parents are only curtailing their effectiveness as trainers because counting again forces them to be objective about their child. Their child does not cry and scream all of the time; he only does so before dinner (when he's hungry?), when baby brother is around (wants attention?), or before bedtime (manipulating Mother in order to stay up?). Observing and counting tells the parent these things.

Table II contains an easy means for counting how often an adaptive behavior occurs and Table III contains an example of a chart for counting problem behaviors.

Each of the behaviors that is being observed in Table II probably occurs every morning within a half-hour's time, so that time is constant.

In the case referred to in Table III of the number of times a child hits another child, again time must be kept constant. That

TABLE II.

EXAMPLE OF CHART FOR COUNTING FREQUENCY OF REQUIRED BEHAVIORS COMPLETED

Behavior	Mon.	Tues.	Wed.	*Day* Thurs.	Fri.	Sat. & Sun.	Total	
Put on shirt	x			x			2	
Button shirt							0	
Put on pants	x				x		2	
Put on shoes			x				1	
Tie shoelaces		x	x				2—dressing	7
Wash face	x				x	x	3	
Dry face	x				x	x	3	
Wash hands			x				1	
Dry hands		x		x			2—washing	9
Clean fingernails		x					1	
Brush teeth			x	x			2	
Comb hair	x						1—toiletting	4
Total	5	3	4	3	3	2	20	

TABLE III.

EXAMPLE OF CHART FOR COUNTING BEHAVIOR PROBLEMS

Behavior	Sat.	Sun.	Mon.	*Day* Tues.	Wed.	Thurs.	Fri.
Jimmy							
Hits baby	5	2	3	2	4	2	3
Says "NO!"	2	1	1	4	4	4	3
Cries							
Total	7	3	4	6	8	6	6
Time Observed (mins.)	60	60	120	50	60	60	60
Rate (per minute)	1.01	0.5	0.03	0.12	0.13	0.10	0.10

is, you must count for five minutes or sixty minutes or for 120 minutes each day; otherwise a *rate* must be calculated. Rate will be discussed shortly.

Counting Behavior—Duration

Often when observing a particular behavior, it may occur only once, but it may last for a long time. For example, a temper tantrum may last thirty, forty or fifty minutes, but still count as only one occurrence. Therefore, if a person succeeds in cutting the temper tantrums from forty minutes to ten minutes, a frequency count would not show this improvement. In this case a time duration can be taken. In Charles' case, for example, time duration was done.

In another example, if improvement in play behavior or time spent in interacting with another child are the targeted behaviors, then total time spent playing or interacting must be recorded. In school, time spent on academic tasks or time spent day-dreaming may be recorded. Also in the school, as an interesting change, time spent by the teacher in attending to inappropriate behaviors (pushing, talking, being fidgety) can be recorded. Recent evidence along this latter point has suggested that special class teachers spend more time paying attention to nonacademic behaviors than they do to academic behaviors so that observation and recording may also benefit the teacher.

In the home or in the laboratory an independent person can observe a parent interacting with his or her child. Or the parent may observe by videotape what he is doing himself or he may observe what the other parent is doing. Most parents say they are sure they praise their child and are very confident in this belief. Yet, one of the first things that must often be done with parents is to make them aware of the fact that they do not praise their child. By observing oneself carefully (e.g. how often I smile at my child), a person sees how *infrequently* he actually does smile. The phrase "know thyself" holds only too true in many cases.

Rating Parents

Parents can use self-rating scales that can be filled out by themselves or by their spouses. Table IV contains a self-rating scale that can be filled out independently by both husband and wife about each other or even by one of their children. This self-analysis gives the parent the opportunity to be critical of what he does. For example, in responding to "how do I observe my child's behavior?", the parent must think in terms of what has already been presented in this book. He must think of being an objective observer, of actually being aware of what his child does. If the parent says that his child cries a great deal, but upon careful observation sees that the child only cries before meals, the parent is a poor observer. If the parent thinks that he praises his child or spouse a great deal, but upon observing and counting finds out that he rarely does it, he is a poor observer.

TABLE IV.
SELF-RATING SCALE BEFORE TRAINING
(filled out by parent and spouse)

	Well		*Average*		*Poorly*
1. How do I observe my child's behavior?	1	2	3	4	5
2. How do I observe my behavior?					
3. How do I observe my spouse's behavior?					
4. How do I praise my child's behavior?					
5. How do I praise my spouse's behavior?					
6. How do I praise my own behavior?					
7. How appropriately do I use punishment?					
8. How do I ignore bad behavior?					

Often having the spouse or child fill out such a rating scale on the mate or parent may show that what the person thinks is praising is not perceived as praising by the supposed recipient. This knowledge forces a reassessment of what is in fact occurring. As a very real example, if a child is promised some money for completing a task, but upon completion he must coerce the parent to give it, and only then is the money given grudgingly, the child cannot see this as being positive. Or if a parent says, "Yes, that's a good job, but your brother would have done it this way, or that way, or better," there is no praise. Such qualification of one's praise seriously curtails its effectiveness. If a child is good, say so —no ifs, ands or buts. If a parent must reassess his praising, he may think carefully of opportunities to do so and even practice in front of a mirror in order to sound convincing (the use of video-taping is very effective in this regard) .

Table V contains a self-rating scale for after a program or during a program. This scale serves as a means of telling the parent if he is improving (or not) and is usually reinforcing for him.

TABLE V.
SELF-RATING SCALE AFTER TRAINING

	Worse	None	Little	A Aver-age	More Than Average	Much
1. Have I improved in observing my child's behavior?						
2. Have I improved in observing my own behavior?						
3. Have I improved in observing my spouse's behavior?						
4. Have I improved in praising my child's behavior?						
5. Have I improved in praising my spouse's behavior?						
6. Have I succeeded in using punishment less?						
7. Have I improved in ignoring bad behavior?						
8. Have I improved overall?						
9. Has my family improved overall?						

Counting Behavior-Rate

To compare unequal observation periods you could find a *rate* over time. For the example of the aggressive child, Jimmy, if one observation period was two hours long and the child hit four times and another observation period was six hours long and he hit twelve times, you could not compare the two frequencies (four hits and twelve hits) without taking the amount of time observed into account (two hours and six hours) . To do this, compute the *rate* by dividing the number of times the behavior occurs (frequency) by the amount of time observing. In the above case 4 hits/2 hours = 2 hits per hour and 12/6 = 2 hits per hour. Thus the rate of hitting was the same for the two observation periods. Fill in the rates to complete the following chart.

In a similar way, you could compute and record the percentage of math problems correct or the percentage of times a child came to you when called or the percentage of words properly pro-nounced when the number of trials from one observation to the

TABLE VI.

Observation Period	Number of Times Child Hits	Number of Hours Observing Each Day	Rate per Hour
1	4	2	$\frac{4}{2} = 2$
2	12	6	$\frac{12}{6} = 2$
3	16	8	
4	24	6	

next is unequal. One assignment might have five math problems, another twenty-five, a third nine; one day he may be called fifteen times, the next day three times, etc. Rates and percents are best used when the amount of time observing or the number of observed trials are very different from day to day. Simple frequency is a good measure in most other cases, but you must observe for the same amount of time each day.

The simplest way to count and record the target behaviors is to make a chart which is put in an accessible place, such as taped to the refrigerator, and to enter the behavior each time it occurs. Table VII shows a chart used for recording the number of times a boy hits his sister each afternoon. The behaviors are tallied each time they occur, and a total is entered for the day. Each observation period was approximately the same, one and one-half hours, so a frequency count gives a good picture of day-to-day changes.

TABLE VII.
TARGET: BILLY'S HITTING HIS SISTER EACH AFTERNOON

Day	Time Observed	# of Hits	Day	Time Observed	# of Hits
1	2:30-4:00	7	6	2:30-4:00	7
2	1:45-3.00	3	7	2:00-3:30	5
3	2:30-4:00	2	8	1:45-3:00	8
4	2:00-3:30	9	9	2:30-4:00	4
5	2:00-3:30	8	10	2:30-4:00	6

Graphing

To visually compare change in a behavior over time, it is helpful to graph the data on the pinpointed behavior you have observed. For the above example recording the number of times the boy hits his sister, the graph would look like Figure 1.

Time is always shown on the horizontal axis and the behavior is shown on the vertical axis. Enter the data for days seven through ten (found in Table VII) on the graph yourself.

By pinpointing the problem behavior and systematically observing, counting, charting and graphing it over a period of time, you get an objective record of how strong the behavior is and how frequently it occurs. Many parents think that a problem is much more severe than it really is. For example, a parent who felt her child had tantrums all the time systematically observed and recorded his behavior for a week and found he had only one tantrum. Likewise a problem could be *more* severe than the parent suspected. Also by recording the behavior before you introduce any program changes or *interventions,* you get a record of the

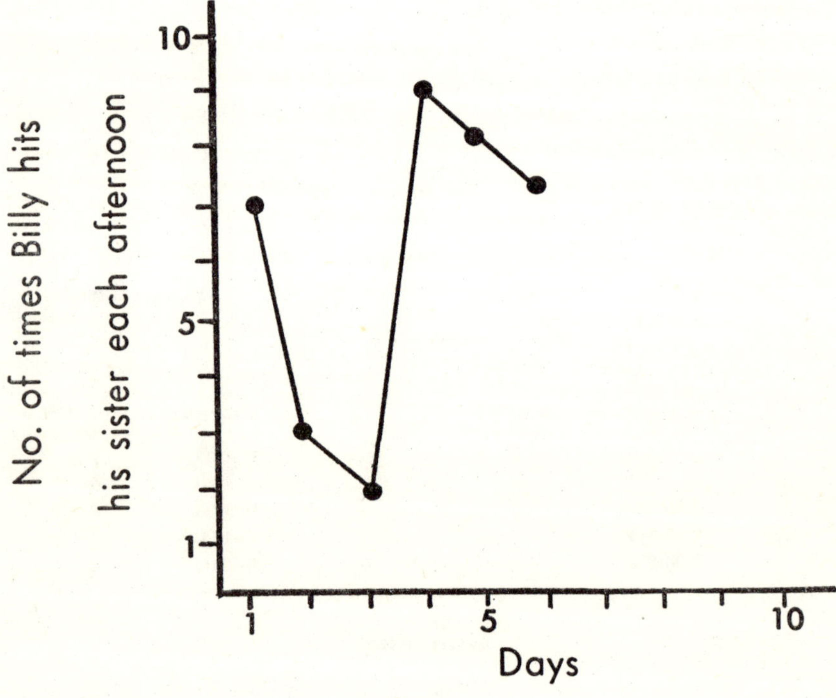

Figure 1.

baseline strength of the behavior. The baseline strength can better be compared with data collected after intervention, and you can thereby have a measure of the success of your program. If the behavior does not change even though a program was introduced, the program should be re-evaluated and probably changed. Also, small improvements which you probably would not notice if you were not charting become more obvious on the graph. For example, in toilet-training a child, if he has an average baseline frequency of twelve accidents a day and then a program is introduced and he has eight or nine accidents a day, his behavior is significantly improved, although you might still feel you are cleaning up after him all the time. The graph would show you that you are having success. In addition, pinpointing and charting make you aware, sometimes for the very first time, of what is actually occurring, structuring your observation of the problem so that eventually you can change and control the behavior.

In summary, when pinpointing your first problem, try to select one which occurs a few times a day. First, observe your child for a few days to see what it is that he does that you consider to be inappropriate. Write these behaviors down on a list. You should also pinpoint the opposite appropriate behaviors that you wish the child would do instead. For example, the pinpointed behavior for a "dependent child" might be grabbing onto mother while she is cooking dinner. The opposite good behaviors might be playing with his toys, watching T.V., or setting the table.

The next step is systematically observing and counting the pinpointed behavior for a baseline period. Make a chart to help you tally the data. Keep the chart in a convenient place. Observe for the same time period every day and observe at the same time as well. For the above example of the dependent child the chart is shown in Table VIII. The pinpointed behavior should also be entered on a graph. Figure 2 illustrates the data in Table VIII.

TABLE VIII.
**TARGET: BOBBY'S GRABBING ONTO MOTHER WHILE SHE IS
COOKING DINNER**

Day	Number of Grabs	Comments
1	6	Stopped when I told him to for a minute only
2	4	Watched T.V. until he saw me cooking
3	7	Started crying when I dropped pan
4	5	Brought his toys to me
5	4	Watched T.V. in kitchen

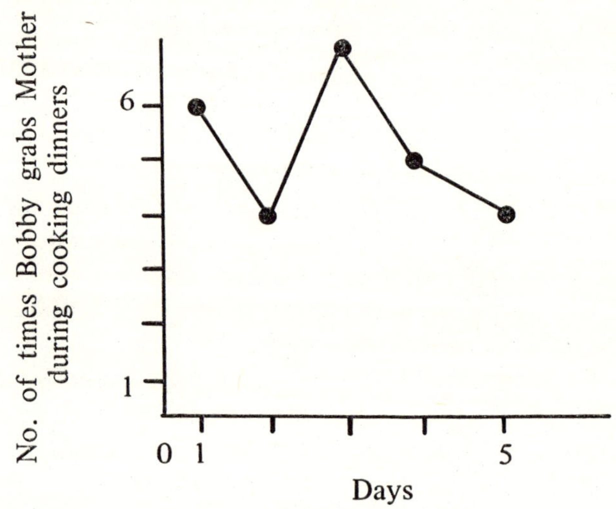

Figure 2.

Home Assignments*

1. Describe one problem you have with your child.
2. Pinpoint that problem by describing specific behaviors.
3. Pick one of those specific behaviors and describe how you would count it.
4. Count, chart and graph that behavior every day for a week (or a day or two days) .

*Use graph paper to visually display your results.

5. Count the number of times your husband ignores your son's (or daughter's) request for attention. The requests may be a question (Dad, do you know . . .? or a statement (Dad, I did . . .) .
6. Count the number of times you ignore a request for attention.
7. Record the length of time you do not speak to your child when he or she is around.
8. Record the number of times you smile within a given period.
9. Fill out a Self-Rating Scale for yourself (see p. 19) .
10. Have your spouse rate you (see p. 19) .

CHAPTER III

INTRODUCTION TO REINFORCEMENT

AFTER YOU HAVE PINPOINTED the problem behavior, observed it, and counted it over a period of time, you are ready to introduce methods to change your child's behavior. The methods that will be discussed are all based on one principle: *Almost all behavior is learned*. Whether you are considering *appropriate behaviors* such as speech, feeding oneself, or working at tasks independently, or *inappropriate behaviors* such as tantrums, fighting or whining, they are all learned, directly or indirectly, from other people. In the case of the child, the parent is probably the most important teacher, although friends, brothers and sisters, and schoolteachers are also involved.

The problem child acts the way he does not because he was born that way, but because he has learned to behave that way. This does not mean that the parent deliberately tried to teach a child to be bad, but many things parents say and do have unexpected results. Children learn to whine and cry each night before they go to bed, dawdle and be late for breakfast each morning, or have temper tantrums every hour. Parents do not want the child to do such things; however, observing what parents *do* when they interact with their child shows that inappropriate behaviors are in fact what they are "teaching."

The child, on the other hand, also trains his parents to nag, scold, and even to spank him! These are certainly not the parent behaviors of the child's choice. Nevertheless, he trains his parents to display problem behaviors.

In interacting with other people, both we and the other person are changed to some degree. In the typical family situation, the parents manipulate each other and their children; the latter in turn manipulate their parents, but most do not know they are being manipulated or that each person is himself an agent of manipulation.

By observing behavior and its *consequences,* that is what happens after the behavior occurs, the family members will be better able to understand what they are teaching each other and will be able to control what behaviors are being learned.

BASIC PRINCIPLES

There are ways to increase adaptive behavior and there are ways to decrease maladaptive behavior. Table IX contains a summary of ways to change both types of behavior. The most common means of increasing adaptive behavior is to reinforce it positively. We can reinforce a child's use of a spoon to feed himself not only through allowing him to eat more but also through praising him. Such reinforcers as food or drink are called primary reinforcers. Praise or a smile or a hug are called secondary reinforcers because they derive their power to increase behavior through being associated, at some time or another, with the administering of a primary reinforcer.

The use of positive reinforcement is the best possible way to strengthen a child's behavior. The removal of a feared object or negative reinforcement (e.g. removal of a slap or the threat of a strap) is another way, but this latter method has been shown not to be as effective as positive reinforcement.

There are also ways to decrease maladaptive behaviors in the behavior-problematic or mentally retarded child. Too often with these children, emphasis has been placed on punishment's being administered indiscriminately, either through slapping, shocking, or physical restraint. However, the most effective means of decreasing the number of times a child screams is to ignore the screaming. This process is called extinction. Another way is to physically remove the child from the environment which he enjoys and which is reinforcing him for this behavior. For example, a verbally aggressive child in a special class may behave in this way because his peers applaud him; or it may be that the use of aggressive behavior is the only way that he can get the teacher to attend to him since he cannot impress her with his academic prowess. Research along this line shows that teachers in special classes respond approximately only 30 per cent of the time to academic behaviors, but almost 70 per cent of the time to maladaptive behaviors (e.g. talking out, getting out of seat). This child may be isolated from his peers so that his aggressive behavior would no longer be reinforced.

Another means of extinguishing maladaptive behaviors is through the administering of punishment. In most cases punishing a child is the worst way either to extinguish his maladaptive behavior or to improve his adaptive behavior. It is much more effective to catch him being good and to positively reinforce him for being good so that he sees that being good pays off.

TABLE IX.
COMPARISON BETWEEN REINFORCEMENT AND PUNISHMENT

Procedure	*Consequence*		*Target Behavior*
	Positive	Negative	
Reinforcement	Applied (e.g. food)	Removed (e.g. release from time-out)	Strengthened
Punishment	Applied (e.g. slap given)	Removed (e.g. food removed)	Weakened

In the present section we will discuss both positive and negative reinforcement. In subsequent sections we will discuss the ways in which reinforcement should be used as well as the use of punishment.

Reinforcement—Positive Reinforcement

Much scientific research, as well as everyday observation, has shown that the consequences following a behavior determine how often the behavior will occur in the future. Thus, if the consequences following a behavior are pleasant or rewarding to the person, the behavior will likely be repeated in the future. This is the basic principle of *reinforcement*. For example, if a child is given a quarter after he mows the lawn, it is likely he will mow the lawn again. The behavior, lawn-mowing, is strengthened or reinforced. and the quarter is the *positive reinforcer* or reward. If a child has a temper tantrum and his mother rushes over to him and makes a fuss for him to stop, the temper tantrum behavior is probably being reinforced by the mother's attention, a positive reinforcer; the behavior is accidentally reinforced. Any behavior that is strong, one that is repeated often, is being maintained by some reinforcer that we may not even recognize. You must look carefully at the consequences of the behavior to determine exactly what the reinforcer is that is maintaining the behavior.

Reinforcement—Negative Reinforcement

Another way to strengthen or reinforce behavior, other than giving something positive or rewarding as described above, is to remove something *aversive,* painful or unpleasant to the person. This is the principle of *negative reinforcement* (not to be confused with punishment, which weakens behavior). The following is an example of negative reinforcement. The child may be misbehaving, having a tantrum, teasing his brother, playing with his food, or anything else the parent finds unpleasant; the parent yells at the child to stop or hits him; the child stops for now, but the parent "sees" that yelling or hitting is effective and the parent is reinforced. For the child, the aversive or unpleasant condition is removed. But the parent will use yelling and hitting again. However, the parent is falling into what has been called the *"criticism trap."* The child's behavior is only temporarily stopped (as we shall see later when we discuss punishment) and he will misbehave again, and the parent will have to yell and hit again to try to make the child stop. And so on and on; each time the parent will have to yell louder to have the same effect of stopping the child from misbehaving. The "criticism trap" is especially dangerous in households where parents use very little positive reinforcement; the major way the child has to get parental attention is through misbehaving. To help get out of the trap, the parent must use a lot of positive reinforcement of the child's appropriate behaviors.

In a similar way, negative reinforcement operates in teaching an aggressive child to hit others. If another child is doing something which the aggressive child does not like, which is aversive to him, however mildly, the aggressive child hits. Most likely the other child will stop the behavior which the aggressive child considered aversive. Thus the hitter learns by hitting to change things that are unpleasant for him. In a similar way, a child's temper tantrum removes the "unpleasantness" of his parents asking him to do his chores; they no longer ask so as not to "upset" him even though, as a result, they are defeating their attempts at training him to be socially independent.

From the principle of reinforcement, we now know that the way to strengthen a behavior is either to apply something positive or to remove something aversive. However, that which is reinforcing for one person might not be reinforcing for another. The only way to tell if something is a reinforcer is to try to use it to strengthen a behavior; if the behavior it follows is strengthened, it was a reinforcer; if not, try again with another possible reinforcer. This is another reason why data collection is so important. The data would show, almost immediately, the effects of a particular reinforcer.

Classes of Positive Reinforcers

I. *Tangible or Material Reinforcers*—Objects of anything material that can be given to the child; most effectively used when paired with social reinforcers; e.g.

candy
doll
new dress
toy truck
comic book

II. *Social Reinforcers*—Reinforcers found in the behavior of other people; probably the most useful reinforcer; the child might have to be taught with tangible reinforcers paired with the social reinforcers; social reinforcers include:

a. expressions
   smiling
   winking
   nodding
   clapping

laughing
looking interested

b. praising words and phrases
good
I love you
you should show that to your father
I'm proud of you

c. nearness
walking together

d. talking and listening to each other
playing with your child
eating together

e. physical contact
touching
hugging
holding hands
patting head
kissing

III. *Symbolic or Token Reinforcers*—Reinforcers that in and of themselves have no value but can be later traded in for a variety of other types of reinforcers. Symbolic reinforcers include:

money
tokens
grades
poker chips
Blue Chip® Stamps
check marks

The child has to learn to find these reinforcing.

IV. *Activity Reinforcers*—A *preferred activity*, one which the child already does frequently and seems to enjoy, can be used to reinforce a less preferred activity or behavior; activity reinforcers can be either things that usually occur during the day or special privileges. Some activity reinforcers are:

watching T.V.
playing with toys

helping to make dinner
eating dessert
staying up late
saying grace
going first
running errands
taking care of a pet
going to a movie
having a party
going on a special trip
choosing what's for dinner

The way activity reinforcers can be used is to require that a weak behavior that seldom occurs, such as hanging up clothes, eating vegetables, or studying, be performed *before* the child has access to the strong preferred activity. Thus, the child has to earn the good things in life. The child first hangs up his coat, and then gets the afternoon snack; first he eats his vegetables, and then he gets dessert; first he studies, then he watches T.V.

In order to change behavior through the systematic use of reinforcers, we must make sure that the appropriate behavior we want to strengthen is being reinforced and that we are not accidentally reinforcing inappropriate behaviors. Are you ignoring him when he tries to feed himself and do you usually feed him yourself because it's easier? Do you give him what he wants before he asks or even if he does not say the words clearly? Is he ignored when he is playing alone and only given attention when he "hangs" on to Mommy? Is he thanked for doing his chores?

The only way to change behaviors is to observe and chart the behavior and its consequences and then to try to arrange the consequences so that appropriate behavior is being strengthened and inappropriate behavior is being weakened. As we proceed through the sessions, specific techniques for changing behaviors will be discussed in detail.

HOME ASSIGNMENT

1. Observe the consequences of the pinpointed behaviors you are observing in your child. Be specific in what you think the re-

inforcers are.

2. List possible tangible, social, token and activity reinforcers for your child.

TABLE X.

Tangible	Social	Token	Activity
1.	1.	1.	1.
2.	2.	2.	2.
3.	3.	3.	3.
4.	4.	4.	4.
5.	5.	5.	5.
6.	6.	6.	6.

3. (a) Order each of the categories in Number 2 as to preference for your child; (b) then order each of the reinforcers within each category according to your child's preference.

4. (a) An infant's getting a hug after saying his first words, (b) a salesman being given a commission on his sales, (c) a child receiving an A on a test, (d) a baby being given a bottle when he cries, (e) a child dressed by his mother so he will not be late for school, (f) a student going to recess after he finishes his math problems, (g) a husband discussing his work problems with his interested wife are all examples of positive reinforcement. List the behavior and reinforcer for each of the above examples.

1.	5.
2.	6.
3.	7.
4.	

A BRIEF RECAPITULATION

IN THE PREVIOUS TWO CHAPTERS you have pinpointed several maladaptive behaviors and kept a record or graph of these behaviors. Graphing allows you to have an objective account of the type of problem and its frequency of occurrence per hour or per day or per week. Thus, when you begin to set up *programs* to change these maladaptive behaviors, you will have a ready *baseline* with which to compare your *success* or *failure*. In the past you have observed a steady increase in the problem behavior over time, i.e. each hour or day the frequency has shown a steady increase, as in Figure 3.

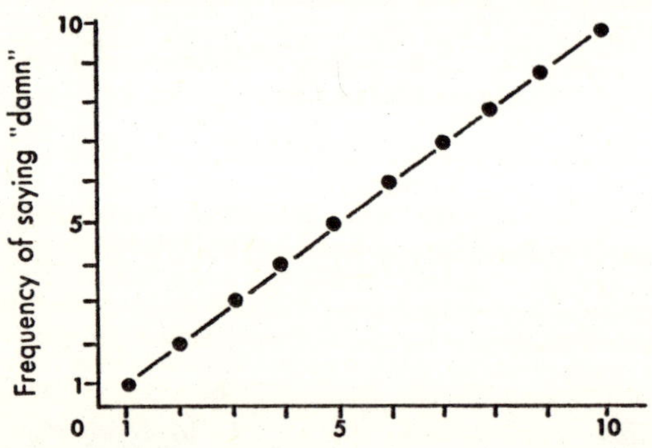

Baseline observations (each equals 1 hr. per day immediately after school for example)

Figure 3.

Once you have instituted a program to *suppress* (weaken) the problem behavior, you may see no immediate *decrease* in the frequency of occurrence; this does not mean that you have *failed*, because what you have done has stopped an escalation of the behavior. Your curve might now look like that in Figure 4.

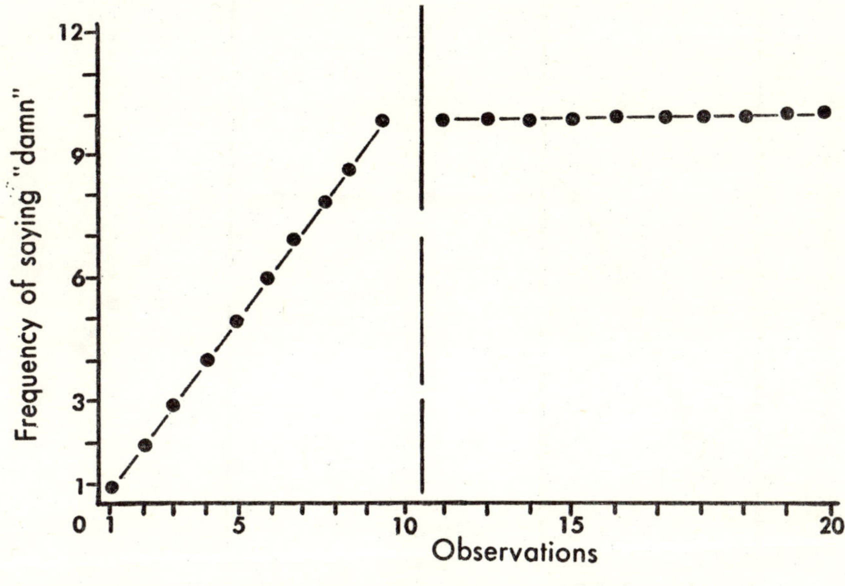

Figure 4.

On the other hand, you may still observe a slight decrease in the frequency, i.e. a *slowing* down or *deceleration* in the frequency so that instead of hearing "damn" once for each hourly observation, you may hear it once each two hours. Again you have succeeded, at least in part (see Figure 5).

The problem behavior may not be decreasing in frequency as quickly as you expect for several reasons.

1. The behavior is too strongly embedded as a part of the child's behavioral pattern *(behavioral repertoire)*. That is, he has been allowed to say "damn" for so long without any negative *consequences* being placed on his saying it, that he has *learned* it well and may *suppress* it slowly. You may recall from the previous chapter the point that parents sometimes aid children in the learning of some maladaptive behaviors by not suppressing them immediately

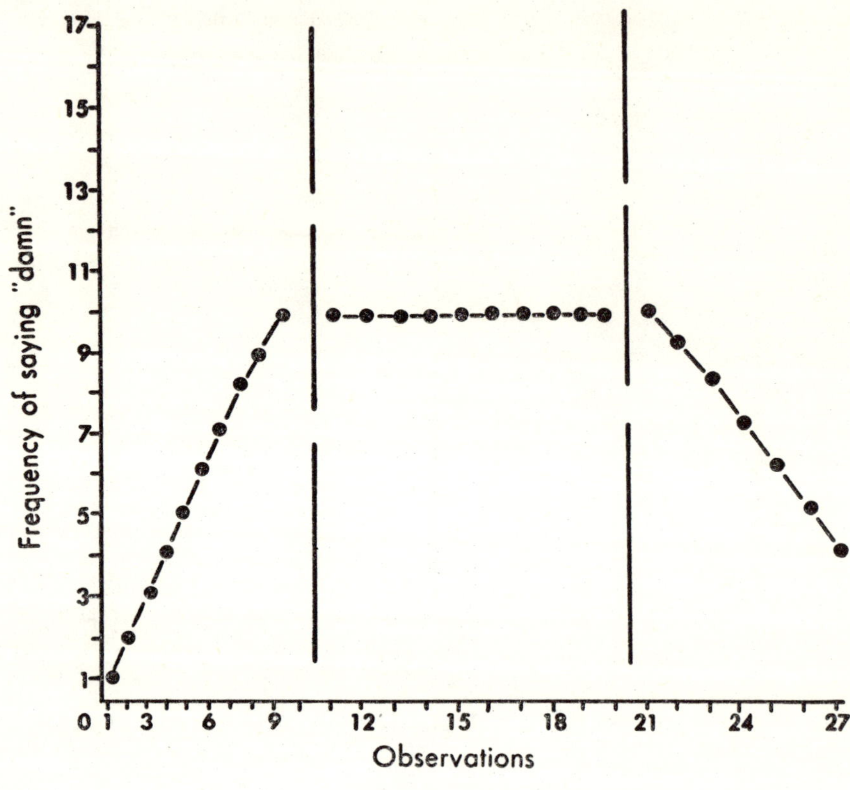

Figure 5.

or by encouraging these behaviors, at least implicitly, as you will see in Case 1.

2. The program may be inadequate. For example, only a *timeout* procedure may have been used. If the behavior is a particularly strong one, timeout alone may be inadequate. It may be necessary to *reinforce* the child when he does not swear or it may be necessary to have him perform a *competing response,* the reasoning being that if he is doing something else, he cannot be swearing.

3. The program may be adequate, but it is not being followed *consistently.* As you will see in Case 1, the father was inconsistent in his suppression of swearing.

More probably you will see a steady decrease in the frequency of the problem behavior. The points mentioned above were meant to show you that difficulties do arise and to encourage you to be as careful as possible in following programs.

The above alternatives may be interpreted from your accurate graphing or recording of the child's behavior. You can see if the program is not working and can take steps to change it *immediately*, before another maladaptive behavior can be learned. Or you can see if your program is succeeding and you can go on to another behavior and can genuinely feel a sense of satisfaction with your efforts.

You can now readily see the need for accurate *pinpointing* of the behavior you want to change—you have to be *explicit* in what it is. The behavior has to occur often enough; you have to observe carefully what immediately precedes the problem behavior and what immediately follows it. This is the process of *identification*.

CASE 1

A boy of five swore consistently at home and at kindergarten, so that the teacher was considering removing him because of the child's effect upon the behavior of other children. The interview with the parents showed that the child could be considered to be a mommy's boy, seeing his father only in the evenings and weekends. The father swore occasionally and was a *social model* for his son. It was also found that when the boy first began to pick up words frequently used by others, "damn" was one of them. When he first spoke the word, both the father and mother smiled and laughed, both potent reinforcers for the boy; soon his saying "damn" was a joke. When the parents' friends came over, they treated it as a joke as well. The friends held him on their knees and often asked the boy to say the word.

When the child went to kindergarten, the teachers did not treat it as a joke. They were shocked because the boy had learned the one word; he was also learning other swear words and generalizing their usage from the home to outside the home.

Only then did the father realize that a home-accepted behavior was not a socially-accepted behavior and attempted to extinguish the swearing. One time when the teacher called about the boy's swearing, the father gave his son a half-hearted spanking; but the father still occasionally laughed at the swearing. The child got *mixed messages* which tended to confuse him at first, but he did *discriminate* when he was supposed to swear and when not to. He swore at home, but not at kindergarten. What happened when he changed schools? He swore again in both places, and this time the teacher had a difficult time getting him to stop at school—the child's behavior had become too strong.

This process is really a *chain* of events, with each part of the chain dependent on the preceding event. Table XI contains a diagram of what went on with the boy in Case 1 and what might have happened if the father had handled the boy differently. If you are observing carefully, you might see that the child swears only when the father is present, and that the father hugs the child immediately afterwards, not necessarily because he likes swearing, but because he is happy to see his child. Unwittingly, the father may also reinforce the swearing.

On the other hand, you may notice that if the child is doing something pleasant or reinforcing to him when the father comes in, the swearing is not elicited by his seeing the father. Still the father is happy to see the child and pats him; here the father reinforces playing behavior. And in this case, playing is a *competing behavior* for the child because it competes with swearing. If a behavior is ongoing, it will generally continue to be ongoing, and it is difficult to have the child do something else—all mothers see this when they try to get the child to wash for dinner when he is playing.

By *systematic analysis* of what is going on, you may distinguish between what *elicits* the problem behavior and what *inhibits* it and can set up a program whereby the inhibiting program is in operation until the problem behavior is *suppressed*.

You may find it useful to use such a table of identification for each problem behavior. In each table, list each of the events leading up to the problem behavior (the antecedent) and that which follows (the consequence). Such documentation provides you with finer and finer ideas of what is occurring.

This *identification* is different from the *pinpointing* and *recording* (graphing) of the frequency of occurrence of the problem behavior. This analysis provides you with a means for *manipulation* so that you can change the frequency. Such manipulation can be in the antecedent stage or in the consequent stage, separately or together.

TABLE XI.

Preceding Events or Antecedents	Problem Behavior	Following Events or Consequences	Problem Behavior
Father comes in – child sees father →	"DAMN" →	Father laughs, hugs him →	swearing reinforced, and strengthened
Father comes in – child playing, does not see father immediately →	child looks up smiles, too engrossed with toys to swear, goes back to play →	Father says hi – pats him on head →	play behavior and smiling both reinforced and strengthened
Father comes in →	Child swears →	Father ignores child →	swearing weakened
Father comes in →	Child swears →	Mother says no; Father ignores child →	swearing weakened

IDENTIFICATION OF ADAPTIVE BEHAVIOR

Usually when a parent sees a child's behavior as a problem, the problem has reached such a point as to be greater than the parents' tolerance of the frustration threshold. When this occurs, the parent tends to ignore all of the adaptive things that the child does and to concentrate on the problematic ones. The difficulty with this kind of emphasis is that the adaptive behaviors may go unreinforced and may be extinguished while the parent is trying to change the problem behavior.

Sometimes it is difficult to be objective when one is faced with an overwhelming problem behavior, but identification of the problem behaviors forces you to think critically and to take time to analyze each of the components of a behavioral chain or pattern. If you emphasize badness, to the exclusion of goodness, taking goodness for granted, you run the danger of having only "badness" being associated with the child. On the other hand, if you make a list of the "good" things that your child does, you may observe that your worry is way out of proportion to the problem.

However, in some cases parents will find a shelter in the thought that he does one thing well; therefore, he cannot really be that bad. This parent fails to realize the implications of his child's behavior just as surely as does the parent who emphasizes only the bad things.

The importance of outlining adaptive behaviors lies in the fact that this allows you to establish a behavioral repertoire. The frequency of occurrence of such a repertoire then aids you in establishing competing responses which you can reinforce, while you can extinguish the problem behavior by nonreinforcement.

For each child, then, you should have not only a list of the problem behaviors, but also a list of the adaptive behaviors. Table XII has some examples of adaptive behaviors.

Most children, even problem ones, have some adaptive behaviors. Reinforcement programs should take both adaptive and problem behaviors into consideration.

TABLE XII.
EXAMPLES OF TYPES OF ADAPTIVE BEHAVIOR

Gets up when first called	Reads books
Washes face by self	Watches television
Dresses self	Plays well with others
Feeds self	Does homework
Cleans room, makes bed	Goes to bed on time
Ties shoes	Speaks clearly
Brushes teeth	Is polite in speech
Plays well by self	

HOME ASSIGNMENT

1. Make a list of all of the things your child can do.

TABLE XIII.
THINGS CHILD DOES

Well Without Help	*With Help*	*After Much Nagging and Help*	*Will not Do at all*
1.			
2.			
3.			
4.			
5.			
6.			

2. Use the following form as a means of stating and identifying the behavior problem and how it is maintained (i.e. the consequences). Use the form for each problem behavior.

NAME: DATE:

CHILD'S NAME: CHILD'S AGE:

1. What is your major problem with the child?
2. What does he do exactly (behavioral definition)?
3. When does this usually occur?
4. How often does it happen? How long does it last?
5. What happens to him after he does it? What do you do? What does Father do? What do siblings do? Others?
6. Does anything seem to affect the behavior? Anything you or anyone else does?

7. How is he usually rewarded? For what is he rewarded? How does he react?
8. How is he usually punished? For what is he punished? How does he react?
9. What are some other problem behaviors that he exhibits?
10. Being the mother of this child makes me feel . . . . . .

CHAPTER V

RESTRUCTURING THE ENVIRONMENT TO CHANGE MALADAPTIVE BEHAVIOR

THE LAST CHAPTER was a review of pinpointing and reinforcement with some added information on each. This next chapter deals with restructuring the environment as a means of changing maladaptive behavior.

As was pointed out earlier, you can manipulate either the antecedents or the consequences of the problem behavior. Let us now deal with manipulating the antecedent events.

For example, Gordon is enuretic in school but not at home. Gordon is mentally retarded but has no physiological reason for being enuretic. The fact that he is differentially enuretic at home and at school suggests that the problem is specific to the school. The mother indicated that she had told Gordon, thirty minutes after each meal, to go to the bathroom. The child did not *attend* to his full bladder because his mother did it all for him.

The warning was *noncontingent,* that is, it came whether or not his bladder was full, so he could not learn to *associate* bladder pain with his mother's warning, and he could not associate relief with emptying his bladder if there was no urgency to his urination. At school, he had no warning stimulus and urinated whenever his bladder was full. So, by simply adding a warning factor at school *(changing the environment),* he soon was no longer enuretic at school.

Another example of the importance of antecedent events was observed by a worker at the home of a distraught mother. The mother had sought help for dealing with her daughter's temper tantrums. Upon careful observation, the observer noticed that each time the mother asked the girl to do something while she was watching television, which filled a great part of her nonschool time, the child did not respond. As the mother continued speaking and was ignored, she became more distraught until, in a fit of anger, she shut the television off which then immediately *elicited* or precipitated a temper tantrum in the girl.

Antecedent	Behavior	Consequence
Mother		
TV on — mother asking question →	Child ignoring mother →	Mother getting madder
Mother shutting TV off →	Girl throws temper tantrum →	Mother hits girl

Figure 6.

This particular chain of events is often seen in homes; in this case, by telling the mother to time her statements for when the child was not attending to something else (the TV or playing), the message was relayed to the child. In cases like these, a competing response (television watching) was curtailing the mother's effectiveness.

There are many more examples such as these which simply involve using a critical eye to determine the problem behavior and what it is that precedes that behavior. Sometimes the *Significant* antecedent event is one which occurs immediately prior to the problem behavior, as in the case of turning the TV off. In other cases, the significant antecedent may be further removed, as in the case of the enuretic.

Other examples of changing the environment to effect behavioral change are

1. Removing all of the districting stimuli (toys, playmates) other than the relevant stimuli, (reading books or spelling). This works particularly well when a child will not attend to a task at hand.
2. Removal of child from the table while others eat if he up-

sets routine *(time out).* Have him watch and eat later *(delay of reinforcement).*

If environmental manipulation alone does not work or if you desire a quicker response to your program, you can also manipulate the consequences of the problem behavior using reinforcement either together with manipulation of the environment or by itself. Generally, combining manipulation of both the environment and the consequences provide the stronger program.

HOME ASSIGNMENT

Antecedent	Behavior	Consequence

Antecedent	Behavior	Consequence

CHAPTER VI

HOW TO REINFORCE

IN MOST FAMILIES reinforcement is usually haphazard and inconsistent. It is haphazard because it is given whenever the significant adult or person who administers the reinforcer attends to the behavior. Reinforcement is often inconsistent because at one time a great deal will be given, and at another time little will be given for the same response. Or reinforcement may be nonexistent, as in the case where adaptive behavior is taken for granted until it is gone. Or reinforcement may be used to strengthen the wrong behavior. For example, if the child performs a task (runs an errand), but enroute does something else (steals some money) and is rewarded, presumably for running the errand, generalization or reinforcement could occur to the other response.

Reinforcement is a powerful tool for each of us in our daily lives, and if it is not used properly it can be ineffectual. As the preceding paragraph indicates, in reinforcing behavior the parent must know what it is he is trying to strengthen, with which reinforcer, and with how much of that reinforcer. This is why an accurate and realistic list of behaviors to be expected of a child must be kept, as well as a list of potent reinforcers.

The easiest way to achieve such accuracy is to keep a chart and to *contract* with the child as to what is to be expected of him and what he will receive in return. Such *behavioral contracting* allows the parent to keep an accurate check on what is done so that he does not miss reinforcing adaptive behavior. It also provides the child with a record of exactly what is expected of him. Do not assume that the child knows what is expected; tell him and run him through the stages if necessary.

In a previous section, reinforcement was briefly described as a means of strengthening behavior. Positive reinforcement is the administering of desirable things; negative reinforcement is the removal of an undesirable thing. In administering either of these, there are definite rules to follow which enhance their effectiveness.

RULES IN USING POSITIVE REINFORCEMENT

1. *In order to be maximally effective, a reinforcer must immediately follow the response you want to strengthen, otherwise you might unwittingly reinforce the wrong response.* For example, if you are working with a child on following commands such as "look at me," or "give me your hand," or "pick up the red block," or if you are having him imitate speech, you must give him the ice cream and hug immediately after he follows the command. If you must dip your spoon to get the ice cream and meanwhile he turns away, you are inadvertantly reinforcing turning away and not the correct response to your command.

A corollary of this rule is, that since in many cases you cannot give him a *primary* reinforcer immediately, you may, however, follow this rule through the use of a *secondary* reinforcer. On the ward on the job, in the class or at home you cannot run around giving a child a candy, ice cream, or a trip to the zoo each time he does something well, but you can give him a token or a star or a check along with your smile and praise in order to bridge the time gap. The child will come to know that receiving the stars means that he can later collect a toy, free time in class, or television privileges with what he has earned. In class, a single checklist can be kept on the corner of each desk, and as work or time spent is completed, checks can be given. At home a "contract" can be kept on the wall, stating what it is the child must do, what the secondary reinforcers are, and what he can later purchase with the secondary reinforcers.

2. *The effectiveness of a reinforcer depends upon its magnitude.* It is commonplace that we work better for a dollar than for a nickel. Similarly, a smile or praise from an admired person means more than one from another person. It follows from this that, in the classroom or on the ward you should determine whether one person or another should work with any one child. Some children work better with men; others with other children.

In addition, we tend to underestimate the effectiveness of social reinforcers with all children, both "normal" children and mentally retarded children. Research by Zigler at Yale has shown that institutionalized retarded children will work for long periods on tasks just to be with another person (the experimenter). One of the most effective reinforcers with the retarded seems to be verbal praise or social interaction, and yet evidence shows that both parents and aides must be taught to praise. As an example, in observing a young, supposedly moderately retarded boy, it was noticed when he did not respond to a question both parents ignored virtually all of his other speech production and finally sought professional help when the boy would only mumble. The answer appeared to be that he enjoyed being with his father, but the only time his father paid attention to him was when the boy failed to do something and then the father criticized him. In this case, both parents had to be trained to praise the boy. Once this was accomplished, the "criticism trap," was broken and the boy spoke in response to his father's praise.

3. *The kind of reinforcer used is important since all children do not work equally well for the same reinforcer.* The same child does not work equally well, all the time, for the same reinforcer. Reinforcers must be individually established. With the children who have failed, or are failing, in academic tasks which are graded with letters (A,B,C), it is illogical to expect them to show an improvement in performance without a change in the reinforcer system. A list for each child can be made, including things he likes to do, things he likes to play with, with whom he likes to play, and what he likes to eat. These can then be given systematically, first for performing tasks, and then for continued improvements in performance.

4. *In order for a reinforcer to be maximally effective a particular child must be familiar with that reinforcer.* For children in an institution, trips to a store or the use of a radio may be too abstract as reinforcers because the children have not experienced them. Similarly, money may be meaningless to some children. In an environment that is devoid of many things, the institutionalized child cannot imagine these experiences. At home it is much

the same thing; promises may not be kept. To counter this, show the child that you will follow through and have the toy or tickets to the zoo already there.

5. *A reinforcer's effectiveness will be enhanced if the child is able to sample it.* Let him hear the radio or see the other children eating, playing, or watching television.

6. *A reinforcer will strengthen a response more if that response is a simple one rather than a complex one.* The command "dress yourself" for a young retarded child is far too complex. The act of dressing can be broken down into first putting on one sock, then another, then a shirt, and then pants. Or at first each of these tasks might be too complex, so that pulling on pants may have to be broken down into having the pants down an inch and then pulled up; down two inches and pulled up. At each stage the child is reinforced, and each stage is shapped into a chain of behavior so that, ultimately, he can perform the entire act.

Shaping his behavior a little at a time is important. Do not expect him to make his bed perfectly the first time. If he has made a bed before, have him at least pull the bedspread up; be flexible, then increase your demands on him progressively so he builds up to the complete expected behavior.

Analyze a task into its component parts. For example, clearing up after dinner to you may be just that, clearing up, but to a child who has not done it before, it means much more. Table XIV has a breakdown of the response making up the total task of clearing up after dinner.

Each of the items in Column C could be broken down even further, but it is not necessary. The point is that each behavior is complex and must be seen as such if reinforcement is to be effective. If a child cannot respond to "clean up," maybe he can respond to "wash dishes" or "clean the table" or "put the dishes away." If he cannot do those tasks, he may be able to "put the silverware away" or "shake the tablecloth," etc. You build into his behavioral repertoire through such shaping, reinforcing him for his best performance *immediately,* each time expecting more of him.

Table XV has another example of a breakdown of a complex

TABLE XIV.
BREAKDOWN OF CLEANING UP AFTER DINNER
INTO ITS COMPONENT PARTS

A *Major Task*	B *Small "Bits"*	C *Smaller "Bits"*
Cleaning up	Cleaning Table	Throwing scraps away Removing dishes Removing tablecloth Shaking tablecloth Putting dishes in sink Filling sink with water
	Washing Dishes	Adding soap to water Washing all well Rinsing all well
	Putting Dishes Away	Drying glassware Drying silverware Putting all silverware in each holder Putting glassware into appropriate place Putting pottery away

behavior into its components. It is a measure of a parent's ability to critically observe and to identify his child's behavior when he

TABLE XV.
BREAKING DOWN CLEANING A ROOM INTO ITS COMPONENT
PARTS

A *Major Task*	B *Small "Bits"*	C *Smaller "Bits"*
Cleaning Room	Fixing Bed	Taking bed apart— **Pulling up under sheet** **Smoothing it** **Shaking pillow** **Pulling up upper sheet** **Smoothing it** **Pulling up bedspread** **Smoothing it**
	Clothes	**Picking clothes up** **Putting clothes in drawer** **Other clothes in closet** **Shoes in boxes** **Dirty clothes in laundry**
	Picking up toys	**Books in shelves** **Toys in boxes**

is able to break down complex behaviors into even smaller behaviors.

To shape a child's eating behavior would involve the establishment of the child's level of responding, a desired response, and a suitable reward. Table XVI has an example of such shaping and its components.

TABLE XVI.
EXAMPLE OF SHAPING EATING BEHAVIOR

Child's Level of Responsibility	Desired Response	Components of Desired Response			Reinforcement
		A	*B*	*C*	
	Eat with utensil	a) Use spoon	Hold spoon in fist Shovel food Get food into mouth at least a little	Pick spoon up Get food on it Hold food to mouth	Eating dinner Words of praise Spoon of ice cream for each response
		b) Use fork c) Use knife			

In Table XVI, if the child could not use utensils but used his hands, you would set up a program in which you would reinforce him for each response from Column C that he made. You would show him how to use utensils several times, praising him and allowing him to eat each mouthful. In extreme cases of retardation, many, many hours must be spent. In other cases, the response is quickly learned and the *secondary reinforcement* is usually potent as the child improves from each segment of the chain to the next one and ultimately to the end. In the present example, eating at the table no longer would be messy or distasteful to the parents. The father would not eat quickly and leave and the mother would not dislike cleaning up the table or the child's clothes. For the child, satisfaction in succeeding, social praise from his parents, and a happier mealtime without scolding would *secondarily reinforce* and thereby strengthen his good eating behavior.

In all shaping sessions, make sure that the child knows what is expected of him and show him if he does not; shape him if he does not attempt to improve. Be consistent in your efforts—if he knows you will back down and let him eat if he just sits long enough, set a time limit. He must try to perform the behavior. Give him thirty seconds on a stopwatch. If he does not, remove him from the table for a few minutes. As he gets better, cut the time down. Shaping eating behavior is depicted in Table XVI.

Where the child must perform certain tasks for certain reinforcers, and if that child is able to understand, the parent may make a *contract* with him. This can be listed and posted on a board and can involve the collection of checks for each behavior adequately done; each check can then be turned in at the end of a week for money. Table XVII is an example of a contract.

TABLE XVII.
EXAMPLE OF CONTRACT

Day	Garbage Out	Room Cleaned
Monday	x	x
Tuesday	x	x
Wednesday		x
Thursday		x
Friday	x	x
Saturday	x	x
Total checks	4	6
Total money paid	20c	30c

Since reinforcers are most effective when given immediately following a response; care should be taken to be immediate. In the case in Table XVII, such a contract would be for older children who would know the value of money and for whom the checks would be secondary reinforcers; that is, they would be just as strong a reinforcer as such primary reinforcers as food. For younger children, the contract may involve getting the nickel each day, right after the garbage is taken out. A check may begin to have value after a child sees them in school.

An issue that is often forgotten by parents is that children *anticipate* reinforcement. If the child knows what he is striving for, he is more likely to do it; if he does not know, he may not try.

INTRINSIC VERSUS EXTRINSIC MOTIVATION

Often parents will state that being so systematic in and dependent upon the dissemination of concrete reinforcers will make the child dependent on getting M & M's® or money each day for the rest of his life. This state of affairs is often called bribery.

To be fair, bribery implies illegality and crookedness, whereas reinforcement is far from illegal or crooked. Reinforcement is practiced daily by our employers. Each of us receives a paycheck every month—this is our own dependency on some external reinforcers of our actions, just as a child may be dependent on our reinforcers. For many of us, however, in addition to the money, there is a genuine feeling of satisfaction at a job well-done, in getting something done early, in the discovery of a new tool, or in the creation of a painting; this is intrinsic motivation. Each of us is reinforced both by concrete reinforcers (food, money) and by less tangible reinforcers such as satisfaction, pride, pleasure.

We do not know how we began to derive pleasure from doing certain things (boating, hunting) ; we cannot always mark a time in our lives when this may have happened. Each of us was, as our children are, only interested in money, candies, TV, or a new bike. Gradually we became aware of some inner satisfaction and so too will our children. For most children the dependence on records, graphs, M & M's, and so on is only temporary. Each child will start to do things, once he is trained, because he will receive good things in return, then he may do some because he wants to please you, then to please himself. The process is slower in some people, but it is always there to some extent.

WEANING FROM IMMEDIATE, CONCRETE AND STEADY REINFORCEMENT

An issue that is related to the development of intrinsic kinds of motivation or reinforcers in children is the issue of weaning the child from dependence upon the parent (or from some significant person always being present) to administer a reinforcer for every adaptive response. Obviously, it is desirable to make the child independent, since the parent cannot always be present at play or at school with the child.

TABLE XVIII.
EXAMPLES OF CONCRETE AND INTANGIBLE REINFORCERS

Concrete (External)		Intangible (Internal)
Primary Reinforcer	*Secondary*	
M & M's	Praise	Satisfaction
Food	Hugs	Pride
Money	Kisses	Pleasure
		Thrill

There are ways to deal with this dilemma, since the ultimate goal is to have the child *generalize* his good or acceptable behavior to circumstances other than those in which they were developed.

One such way is to reinforce a child immediately for *every* response that he makes according to your contract at the beginning. For example, as you shape his eating behavior or lifting of a spoon, he would receive each mouthful, plus your praise. Gradually, however, you would praise him *intermittently,* that is, each second response or every fifth response while you eat. Usually, it is better in the initial training stages that you already have eaten, so that you are not irritable and can pay attention to his efforts.

It has been shown that intermittent reinforcement makes a response more resistant to extinction when reinforcement is completely stopped, more so than does reinforcement for every response. The strength of this finding is that you can spend less and less time on reinforcing one response and still feel confident that it will remain strong, and can go on to another. This also allows you to feel reasonably secure in knowing that the child will continue to maintain the appropriate response, even if you are in the next room. You can try this. Once he can eat reasonably well, let him eat by himself. Go into the next room and come back later. If he has finished within a certain time and has not spilled food on the table or on himself, praise him. In this way you are placing some of the responsibility on the child to do well. If you assume all of the responsibility all of the time, he will be dependent upon you for all *cues.*

The next stage with this child, or even with the child who does well at home but is a behavior problem at school or elsewhere, is to contract with him and the teacher. The teacher provides a record of the child's behavior for the day, and the mother reinforces at home. One danger is apparent in this, however—the teacher may then depend on the parent for all types of reinforcement and discipline of the child. If the contract is made explicit and proceeds to the stage where the child's word is enough, the teacher's role can be curtailed. Again responsibility becomes the child's. Do not accept another child's comments; either observe progress yourself or depend upon some other significant person. The next stage is really a culmination of the two previous stages. As the parent reinforces with concrete reinforcers, he also uses praise and words of encouragement. These are social reinforcers that are used by others in the child's environment as well and provide for a means of generalizing reinforcement beyond the home.

Figure 7 provides a depiction of the various stages through which a child progresses. It must be remembered that such development is progressive in normally developing children. For those children who have developmental problems, the process may be slower or may never reach a Stage V level. We all know people who do things only for money and the comforts money can buy. Retarded children also may have difficulty associating praise with performance and may only do some things always for concrete reinforcers. These are exceptions and not the rule.

Generalization

You will also realize that ordinarily reinforcement does not have to be done for all behaviors you want the child to perform. Usually, he will generalize not only from home to school, but he will also *generalize* from one behavior to another.

This is in the same vein as having the child perform "clean up after dinner." At first he may not be able to perform the whole job, but he can do the dishes. Reinforcing dishwashing will generalize to cleaning the table and to putting the dishes away.

This last point of generalization is very important to remember and be aware of. *If you set up a program where similar responses are required, you will find maximal generalization.* If you

	Behavior	Schedule and Type of Reinforcement	Consequence
STAGE I	Child's response ⟶	Candy given Mother's praise ⟶	Child's response strengthened
STAGE II	Child's response ⟶	Candy given every 2nd time (or 3rd or 4th, etc.) Mother's praise ⟶	Child's response strengthened
STAGE III	Child's response ⟶	Mother's praise only ⟶	Maintains and strengthens child's response even if concrete not given or until one is given later. Delay of reinforcement is progressively increased until the ideal is established, i.e. he may wait two days but three days is too long to wait for getting to watch TV or to go to store or park.

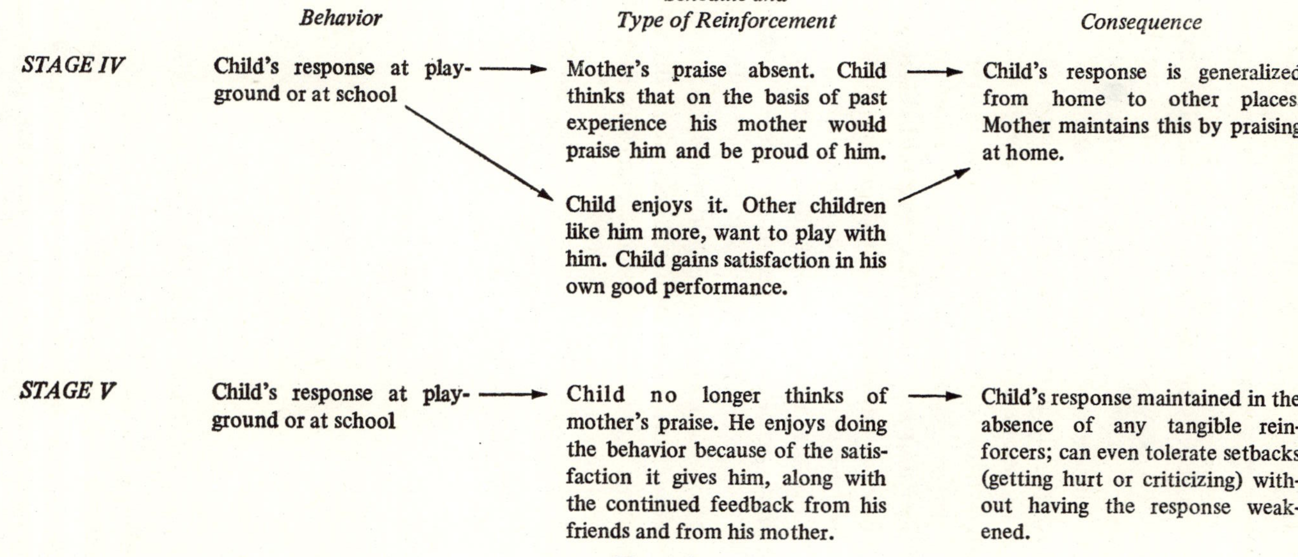

Behavior

Schedule and
Type of Reinforcement

Consequence

STAGE IV

Child's response at play-ground or at school

Mother's praise absent. Child thinks that on the basis of past experience his mother would praise him and be proud of him.

Child enjoys it. Other children like him more, want to play with him. Child gains satisfaction in his own good performance.

Child's response is generalized from home to other places. Mother maintains this by praising at home.

STAGE V

Child's response at play-ground or at school

Child no longer thinks of mother's praise. He enjoys doing the behavior because of the satisfaction it gives him, along with the continued feedback from his friends and from his mother.

Child's response maintained in the absence of any tangible reinforcers; can even tolerate setbacks (getting hurt or criticizing) without having the response weakened.

Figure 7.

have many different responses all required around a period of time the child may not perceive the similarities and will not generalize. This would mean that the parent should block out similar tasks to be done at the same time. For example, all bed making behavior should be at one time, dressing at another, putting toys away at another; do not give him so many messages at one time that he gets confused and does not hear what you really want. (Caution: *Give the child one message at a time until he can tolerate, understand and remember several at a time.*)

The same issue can be raised when trying to decelerate a problem behavior. A temper tantrum is made up of several components as outlined in Table XIX. We will discuss ways in which problem behaviors can be weakened or suppressed later, but the same principle of generalization applies. The child may not respond to "stop the temper tantrum" since the concept is too broad. He may however, respond to "stop crying" along with appropriate reinforcement (praise) for stopping. He may also respond to "stop spitting," since both of these are components of temper tantrums; however, immediately after the child stops crying and spitting, each of the other behaviors may also stop, and thus, generalization has also occurred.

TABLE XIX.
COMPONENTS OF TEMPER TANTRUMS

Crying
Jumping up and down
Hitting
Kicking
Spitting
Throwing things
Swearing

NEGATIVE REINFORCEMENT

Each of the ideas listed so far in this chapter deals with strengthening a behavior through giving a reinforcer when that behavior occurs. This is a positive reinforcer. There are other ways to increase a behavior's strength. One such way is through the removal of something that is threatening or aversive to the child. The child hates arithmetic, talks out, is scolded, and is sent out of the room as punishment. This escape behavior is strengthened; the child does not view being sent out of the room as punishment, but rather as reinforcement because he is getting away from doing arithmetic. Negative reinforcement can work both ways. In a vocational rehabilitation setting the supervisor yells at a young retarded person who then works to stop the yelling. The supervisor in turn sees that his yelling works and his yelling is strengthened, but the man's work behavior is not. Since we build up a tolerance, the next time the supervisor will have to yell louder and longer in order to get the man to work. The supervisor is caught in a trap. He should instead be using positive reinforcers.

Associated with the removal of aversive or undesirable consequences are verbal reprimands which are then secondary negative reinforcers. These verbal reprimands serve the purpose of not having to use actual threats, much in the same way as tokens are used in secondary positive reinforcement.

There may be generalization of the effectiveness of the removal of negative reinforcers. For example, if a particular aide is associated with a child's being locked in the timeout room and the child attempts to escape from her, he may also try to remove himself from all others who look like her. Similarly, he may try to stay away from all activities associated with her. If she is also the one who is training him to dress himself, her effectiveness is gone as a teacher because of his fear of her. She must take steps to become a positive reinforcer by verbal praise at other times, or another person must be used as a teacher.

HOME ASSIGNMENT

1. Work out a behavioral contract for your child for a behavior (e.g. doing homework) that you want improved.

2. List tangible, positive reinforcers for your child and see if you can substitute social reinforcers for them.

3. Break down the behavior that you want your child to learn into its component parts.

	Components of Behavior		
Major Task	Small Bits	Smaller Bits	Schedule and Type of Reinforcement
Behavior I			
Behavior II			

4. Try to break down the "smaller bits" even smaller.

5. Work out a plan to take your child off tangible reinforcers and onto more intrinsic reinforcers. Remember to record and graph to see if you are succeeding.

6. Describe how you might implement continuations of any of your programs to school, to the playground, to visits to relatives as evidence of generalization.

CHAPTER VII

EXAMPLES OF PROGRAMS USING REIN-FORCEMENT FOR IMPLEMENTING A RESPONSE AND/OR ACCELERATING THE FREQUENCY OF THAT RESPONSE

THE FOLLOWING USE practical situations to show development of all of the principles discussed so far. Several cases will be followed through in detail, from identification of the problem through changing the problem behavior.

CASE 2: A SHY POORLY-SPOKEN BOY

Description

Boy, good looking, normal physical development, seven years of age. No neurological problems, no history of retardation, and no emotional disturbance.

Presenting Problem

Mother presented several problems with her son:
1. Excessively shy with strangers. Would bow head and not look at person.
2. Messy at meals, ate with hands.
3. Spoke softly, almost inaudibly.

There is more than one problem involved in the present case. To begin with, shyness and speaking softly were identified as critical problems to work with first, since adequate communication is essential for developing school-related abilities.

EXPLANATION OF A. In a matter of seconds the mother asked the child several important questions without once waiting for the child's response. Finally, she resorted to shame, since no child wants to be inferior to a sibling. This shaming, more importantly,

TABLE XX.
IDENTIFICATION OF PROBLEM BEHAVIOR

Preceding Events/Antecedents	*Problem Behavior*	*Following Events/Consequences*
A. Mother introduced child to observer saying "Say hi to Miss Carson, Ted," "don't bow your head."	Shyness — bowing head when greeting stranger	Bows head, stands close to mother, shuffles feet, opens mouth, shuts it
"Ted's happy to meet you, aren't you Ted?", "Show her your schoolwork." "I don't know what I'm going to do with him, he's just not like my daughter."		Runs from room
B. Mother places food on plate, child starts eating with fingers, everyone begins eating, father notices child's behavior, accuses mother, mother argues and tells Ted to stop, shows him once with spoon, she eats.	Messy at meals	Child continues to eat with fingers, behavior is strengthened. Father's attention appeals to him as he sees little of his father.
C. Child sings to himself, mother tells him to be quiet, then asks him what he is doing, no response, and mother taunts him	Speaks softly	Child will not speak spontaneously, no singing to himself, will mumble when coerced to speak.

was done in front of a stranger, someone who is an unknown. Ted then fled the room.

EXPLANATION OF B AND C. The mother does not adequately train Ted to use utensils. In addition she extinguishes any attempts by him to sing to himself when she yells at him and taunts him.

Behavioral Observation (Baseline)

A. The mother lists important reinforcers to the child, which include interaction with father (sitting on his knee), watching television, chocolate ice cream.

B. Mother lists all the adaptive behaviors the child does,

which include washing self, cleaning room, playing well by himself, playing well others, doing well in school.

C. Mother makes a list of how she responds when the child exhibits the problem behaviors and when he does the adaptive things. She notices some of the observations already listed by the observer and notices that she also takes for granted the boy's adaptive abilities. She mentions how pleased she is to see his schoolwork and to see him playing by himself. She also mentions that she is not an expressive person and anyway she hasn't the time to spend praising him for keeping out of her hair. Now she realizes that she is a contributor to his problem behavior.

D. Mother pinpoints two behaviors: "responding to question" and "speaking softly" and observes both for the three hours, that is, from the time the boy is home after school until the time he is in bed. She records the frequencies on a sheet of paper, as in Table XXI.

TABLE XXI.
FREQUENCIES OF TWO BEHAVIORS

Day	Not Responding to Question	Speaking Too Softly
1		
2		
3		
4		
5		
6		
7		

The mother then plotted these frequencies as in Figure 8 for visual display.

After plotting the frequencies, the mother noticed a relationship between the frequency of occurrence of "speaking too softly" as compared to that of "responding to questions." She observed that as one increased, the other decreased reliably over each of the seven days of observation. She suggested that the two were probably interrelated, which appeared reasonable since they were both verbal behaviors.

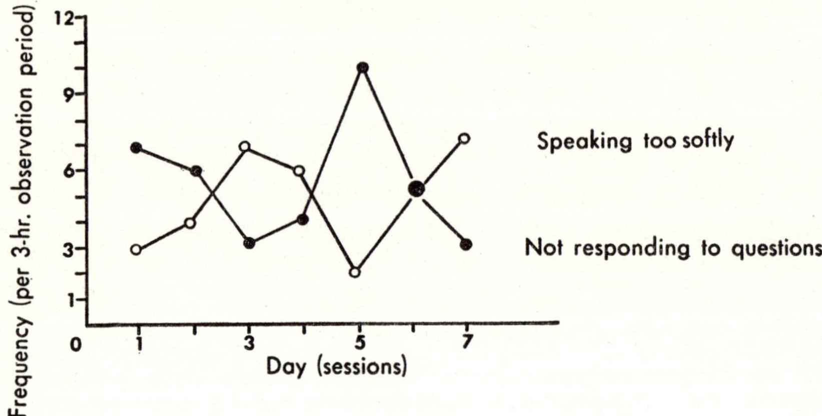

Figure 8.

Programs

Manipulation of Mother's Behavior

In line with her realization that she demanded too many things at once from the boy, the mother planned to change the antecedent behaviors to determine their effect upon the two *target behaviors.*

She decided to ask one question at a time and persist until the child responded to that particular question. She would only speak to the child when he was not performing a competing response (playing, watching television) . She did this for seven days, during which time she kept a record of both target behaviors again. She asked questions for the same number of times as she had the previous week. The frequencies were then plotted, as in Figure 9.

This time the mother found that because she had changed her own behavior (the antecedents) , her son responded to all questions put to him. "Speaking too softly" did not change in frequency, so she set up a reinforcement program to deal with that problem.

Institution of Reinforcement Intervention

The mother's plan was to break down "speaking too softly" into its component parts for shaping purposes and to establish the

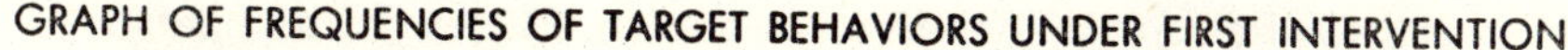

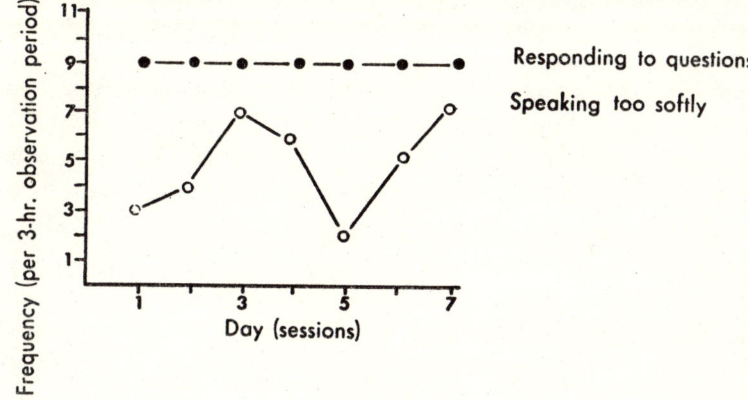

Figure 9.

appropriate reinforcers. She defined speaking loudly as being heard at least five feet away. The components of "speaking too softly" are listed in Table XXII.

TABLE XXII.

Behavior A	Behavior B	Behavior C
Speaking loudly	Forming words soundlessly / Forming words softly / Saying "Ted" / Saying "Mother" / Saying "I want dinner"	Watching mother's lips forming single word / Being heard whispering in mother's ear / Being heard 1 foot away / Being heard 3 feet away / Being heard 5 feet away

Reinforcer: Teaspoon of chocolate ice cream for each correct response.

The mother decided to begin with the easiest response, whereby the mother would use simple words and have the child at least make a sound. She selected "Ted," "Mother," and "I want dinner" as the words to be worked with. She sat the child down at the kitchen table, without any toys around, and as she said each word and the child responded, she said, "Good, but please speak louder," and gave him some ice cream. As the child responded, she moved back further and continued the process. She then began receiving two responses before giving him some ice cream. Soon the child began asking questions spontaneously, speaking loudly, and the mother began washing dishes while still speaking to the child and praising him.

Generalization and Weaning

While the mother moved about the house, the child was generalizing his responding to situations other than those in which he was trained. The child's response also became independent of ice cream and his behavior was maintained by social praise. In addition to situational generalization of responding, the mother and the observer noticed a diminishing of his shyness to strangers. As the mother praised his performance, the child beamed and would often begin speaking spontaneously even to a stranger.

The taking of time for the recording of behavior has an interesting effect in some children. While the parent observes and records one inappropriate behavior, she usually ignores other inappropriate behaviors which then are *extinguished* because reinforcement does not occur. One mother recently mentioned that this occurred in her son whom she was observing for swearing. While she recorded the swearing she did not attend to nosepicking which in the past she used to reinforce by paying attention to the boy. This example points out the useful techniques of ignoring certain behaviors to extinguish them. This technique works only if you ignore consistently; a single instance of attending can reinstitute and strengthen the behavior.

In both of the previous examples, and in the following example, the use of punishment is purposely omitted because removal of privileges or application of punishment is usually the method of discipline most often chosen by parents to the virtual exclusion of more positive measures. The present examples were chosen to point out the lack of punishment procedures since reinforcement often works just as effectively. The next case demonstrates how a mother reinforced a child's "whining" through her paying attention to such behavior in the girl and demonstrates how such behavior can be extinguished through not attending (nonreinforcement or removal of reinforcement) and how to reinforce proper speaking.

CASE 3:   A RETARDED, WHINING GIRL

Description

A moderately retarded girl, nine years old, living at home. Child was born prematurely and may be slightly brain damaged.

Presenting Problem

1. The child continually pesters her mother, hanging around her skirts.
2. The child whines when she speaks; whining defined as a nasal, high-pitched, loud and demanding cry.
3. Throws temper tantrums when not allowed her own way in playing, refuses to follow orders if not to her liking.

Again there is more than one problem behavior, but it appears that they are interrelated.

Explanation

In this case, whining and pestering have become almost synonymous. So much so that probably a program to treat one behavior would automatically effect the rate of the other.

Behavioral Observation

A. The mother lists all effective reinforcers for the child; these include mother's attention, M & M's, dolls.

B. Mother lists adaptive behaviors.

C. Mother makes a list of what she does when the child whines and immediately before the child whines. By taking the time to observe and be critical, the mother notices that each time the child whines, the mother tenses up; as the cry is made a second time, the mother responds and, depending upon her mood, she

TABLE XXIII.
IDENTIFICATION OF PROBLEM BEHAVIORS

Antecedents	Problem Behavior	Consequences
A. Mother picks up child while at sink, puts her down at her feet, talks to child giving her little bits of food. Child talks, asking for more, mother gives it, child demands; mother still gives it. Mother moves to table to write, child moves with her, sits at her feet, demands attention, mother pats her on head, once, ignores second demand, does not correct her. Mother's friend comes in to have tea and talk, child still hangs around, child interrupts, whining continuously, mother gives child a toy or candy to keep her quiet.	Child pesters mother	The child has been effectively shaped and reinforced by the mother to be a whiner and pest.
B. Mother has shaped child to not pay attention to some of her messages. For example, when mother asks child to do something, mother thinks child cannot do it herself, so does it for her. Child has learned that crying gets mother's attention. Mother demands that something be done, child cries louder, mother gives in, hugs child, does thing for child.	Child throws temper tantrums when she does not get her way	Child is conditioned to throw a tantrum when asked to do something, especially if she is doing something else

will either pick the child up before speaking to her or she will just stand there and yell at her. The observer even noticed once that when the mother refused to pick her up first, the child threw a tantrum and then the mother picked her up.

D. Mother pinpoints two behaviors, "whining" and "temper tantrums," and makes a frequency count for seven days three hours each day, as in Table XXIV.

TABLE XXIV.
FREQUENCIES OF TWO BEHAVIORS

Day	Whining	Temper Tantrums
1	/ / / / /	/ / /
2	/ / /	/ /
3	/ / / / /	/ / / /
4	/ / / / / / /	/ / / / /
5	/ / / / / / / / / / / / / / / /	/ / / / / / / / / / / / / / /
6	/ / / / / / / / / / / / / / /	/ / / / / / / / / / / / / / /
7	/ / / / / / / / / / / / / / /	/ / / / / / / / / / / / / / / /

The mother then plotted these frequencies, as in Figure 10.

PLOT OF FREQUENCIES OF PROBLEM BEHAVIORS FOR BASELINE PERIOD

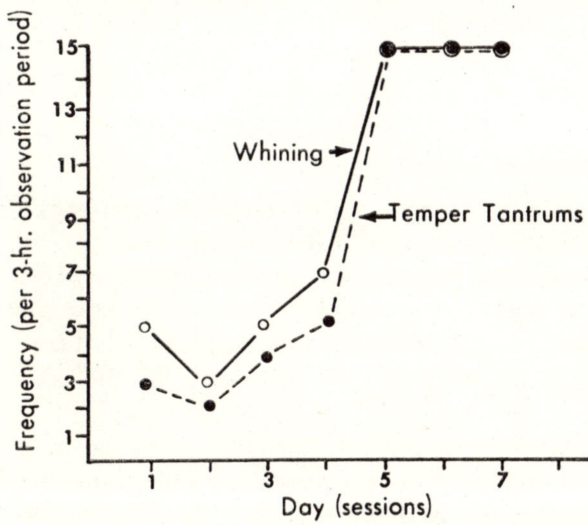

Figure 10.

After plotting the frequencies, the mother noticed that whining and temper tantrums occurred at similar frequencies *and* at similar times; that is, whining always preceded the occurrence of a temper tantrum. The mother further suggested that the conflict between herself and the child built up until the child threw the tantrum and she "backed off." In addition, the mother saw that whining and tantrums were occurring consistently and regularly and were the child's chief means of communication with her.

Programs

Manipulating the Mother's Behavior

Since the mother realized that she provided the antecedent events that preceded the whining and temper tantrums, she planned to literally remove herself from the hearing of the child each time the child called. She would remain observing, but unseen by the child, and would only intervene if the child was in danger of injuring herself. If the whining occurred at dinner, the child was warned once of the consequences, and if the whining occurred again, she was removed from the table.

The mother found that ignoring the child's whining reduced both whining and temper tantrums even on the first day, and for subsequent days the frequency of both was reduced to only about four and five occurrences per day. The mother was recording for the same time period as during the baseline.

Institution of Reinforcement Program

Since whining and temper tantrums were still occurring, the mother decided to continue ignoring whining and to praise the girl each time she spoke nicely or responded nicely to a question. The mother also gave some candy as a reinforcer and made sure she asked the question when the child was not preoccupied with a competing response. On each day of the reinforcement period she asked fifteen questions.

The observer felt, however, that the mother would be more convinced that the decrease in whining was really a function of her changes if she returned to her original way of responding to the child; that is, if she reversed herself.

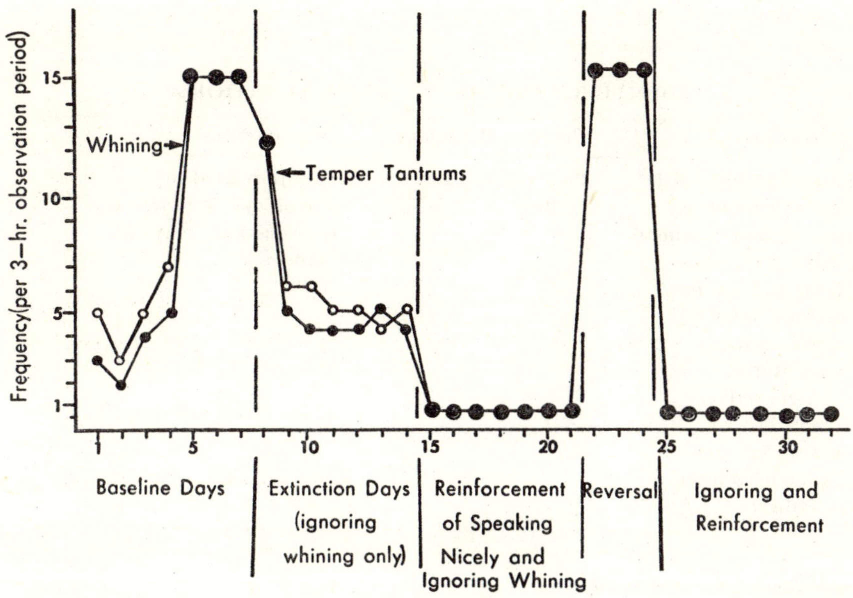

Figure 11.

As the reversal part (D) of Figure 11 indicates, the child immediately began whining and having tantrums again when the mother did not ignore the whining and did not recognize or praise the child for speaking nicely. The child obviously quickly realized that the rules of the game had been reversed and since whining was still a strong behavior, she picked it up again.

The mother then reinstituted the ignoring and reinforcement phases and the child immediately stopped whining and temper tantrums.

CASE 4: AN EXAMPLE OF BEHAVIORAL CONTRACTING

Description

A boy of twelve who was not retarded, but was having difficulty in school.

Present Problems

His chief difficulties were in reading and spelling as listed in Table XXV.

TABLE XXV.
IDENTIFICATION OF PROBLEM BEHAVIORS

Antecedents	*Problem Behaviors*	*Consequences*
Parents had ignored child's demands for appreciation of school-related activities. Father did not have time and valued athletic abilities more. Mother tried to overcome father's lack of interest, but the boy modeled after the father.	Poor reading and spelling	Failure related to school, dislike of school, self-conscious, may fail grade

Behavioral Observations

Upon speaking with mother and father, both now recognized that child was a potential for school failure and that Father had not realized his role in the son's failure. Both agreed to set up a behavioral contract with the boy.

Since the boy's reading and spelling were poor, a tape of his reading a passage was made for the baseline observation, and one of his old spelling papers was used as the spelling baseline observation. The previous reports' grades were also used.

The boy's chief desire was for praise from his father and to spend time with him in athletic activities or in just talking about "men things."

Both the mother and father agreed to orient their behavior so that they would adhere to the contract, and the father would change his schedule so that he could spend time with the boy as the boy improved. The contract was explained to the boy. Each evening he would read segments of stories and he would receive a check for each paragraph read correctly in thirty minutes (correction would be done by one of the parents). Each week he would also bring his spelling paper home from school, and for each correct word he would receive a check. At the end of each week, all checks would be totaled and he could spend them on a list of activities. The contracts are outlined in Tables XXVI and XXVII and a list of activities and costs are in Table XXVIII. In addition, any improvement in a grade in reading or spelling would receive special attention and any perfect spelling or reading performance would get special attention and assigned a star (⋆). The parents gave the spelling test a second time each week, so the child had a great many opportunities to be reinforced.

TABLE XXVI.
BEHAVIORAL CONTRACT FOR READING
(PINNED TO KITCHEN WALL)

Day	Passages Read Perfectly	Errors	Total Paragraphs Read Correctly	Checks
1	0	15	1	/
2	0	12	3	/ / /
3	0	9	2	/ /
4	0	8	3	/ / /
5	1*	0	5	/ / / / /
6	2**	0	5	/ / / / /
7	HOLIDAY		19	19

TABLE XXVII.
BEHAVIORAL CONTRACT FOR TWICE WEEKLY SPELLING TESTS

	Day	Number of Correct From Total of 15	Perfect Papers	Checks
Week 1	1	5		/ / / / /
	2	5		/ / / / /
Week 2	1	7		/ / / / / / /
	2	8		/ / / / / / / /
Week 3	1	10		/ / / / / / / / / /
	2	15	*	/ / / / / / / / / / / / / / /
Week 4	1	15	*	/ / / / / / / / / / / / / / /
	2	15	*	/ / / / / / / / / / / / / / /
		80	3	80 Total

TABLE XXVIII.
COSTS FOR ACTIVITIES*

CHECKS	*STARS*
Basketball game with father = 50 checks	Fishing trip for 2 hours with father = 5 stars
Working on building boat each 30 minutes = 20 checks	Day fishing trip with father = 10 stars
Money—each penny = 1 check	Overnight camping trip with father = *Improved grade in either spelling or reading*
Television each 15 minutes = 15 checks	

*Half of each cost had to come from checks for both reading and spelling so that the boy could not do well in one and be poor in the other.

Results

By keeping records, both the parents and the boy were able to keep track of their behaviors. The parents were locked into a contract on which they had to follow through, while the son had to work to attain those goals. Within a short while, both the behaviors of the parents and the son were such that records were no longer necessary, and the boy was even able to tolerate having to put off a fishing or camping trip with his father. In addition, the boy began to take real pride in school as a direct result of his improved reading and spelling and the additional reinforcement from his teachers.

CHAPTER VIII

WAYS TO WEAKEN MALADAPTIVE BEHAVIOR

THE METHOD OF BEHAVIOR CONTROL that has been stressed thus far has been reinforcement, the process whereby appropriate or adaptive behaviors are strengthened. Now there will be a discussion of ways to weaken maladaptive behavior.

EXTINCTION

Extinction is an alternative to punishment and is the removal of any reinforcement if a child misbehaves. A child who cries each night as he is put to bed, which immediately brings his parents to his side, is reinforced for crying. If the crying is a problem, and not due to some discomfort or medical problem, it will stop if he is put to bed lovingly and then left alone. Usually there is a slight increase in a behavior once extinction begins. Extinction can also be used in the classroom by the teacher's ignoring a child's boisterousness. Head-banging will also decrease in extinction; however, the initial increase in behaviors emitted may cause consternation, so that the most effective plan is to introduce and reinforce an incompatible behavior. The child cannot cry and eat at the same time. The child who bites her arm cannot do so and eat candy at the same time. One way to weaken behavior is through *extinction,* the process whereby a previously reinforced behavior is no longer followed by a reinforcer. The response is weakened through extinction, but it is usually a long process, especially for a response that was reinforced *intermittently* in the past.

There are times when you want to weaken inappropriate or maladaptive behavior, and extinction is not feasible. Behaviors that might require other methods would be those behaviors that (1) are dangerous to the child or others, (2) that occur at such a high rate that no other adaptive behavior occurs, or (3) that are being maintained by reinforcers that are more effective than any reinforcers you can apply for adaptive behaviors. Examples of dangerous behaviors are playing with matches or knives, running into the street, setting fires, or throwing things at others. Examples of high rate behaviors are the head-banging, other *self-stimulatory* behaviors such as those seen in autistic children, or constant fighting as the only means of interacting with other children. Examples of strongly reinforced maladaptive behaviors are taking toys away from other children (having the toy is reinforcing), coming home later from school (being out is reinforcing), or overeating (having food is reinforcing).

For the types of behavior mentioned above, punishment might have to be used to weaken the behaviors. The term punishment refers to specific scientific procedures of behavioral control; just as reinforcement refers to a procedure of following a behavior by a consequence which increases its future strength, punishment refers to a procedure of following a behavior by a consequence which decreases its future strength. One method of punishment involves weakening a behavior through the application of a negative or aversive consequence. This is probably the most widely used and abused form of punishment. Hitting, spanking, scolding, yelling and electric shocking would fall under this type of punishment. Another method of punishment involves the removal of something positive or reinforcing following a behavior to be weakened. Taking away toys, attention, food, privileges, check marks, or money are examples.

Timeout

The procedure of *timeout*, previously mentioned, is an example of this type of punishment; following an inappropriate behavior the child is removed from the social reinforcers that come from being with others. For reasons to be discussed below, the withdrawal of something positive is the preferred method when punishment is to be used to weaken a behavior.

A very effective means of weakening maladaptive behavior is to remove the child completely from a reinforcing environment or to remove the environment from him. This procedure is called timeout and is similar to extinction, except that timeout is instituted immediately or contingently following misbehavior and is terminated once the behavior has stopped. Extinction is usually in effect for a longer period of time and is noncontingent upon the misbehavior. For example, a child who consistently bites herself is placed in a room by herself for several hours each day. Within a few days, the rate of biting has dropped significantly. In this case there has been no contingent removal of attention or reinforcement. This is extinction.

Timeout may take several forms; it may be physically restraining a child with handcuffs, placing him in a room devoid of stimuli, or removing a book so that he cannot read to earn points. Each removal is contingent upon misbehavior; the material is reintroduced after a period in which the child has quieted down. There are numerous examples of timeout. When you are working with a child in speech imitation and he starts to cry, your turning your head away until he stops crying will effectively extinguish his crying. A child may be removed from the food and social reinforcement of the table if he acts up. Eating later by himself, when the food is cold, may deter him from doing this again. A child is loud in class and is lauded by his classmates; removing him from class, to do the work later by himself, effectively stops reinforcement. A child may ignore your instructions while he is watching television; shutting the television off while you explain and keeping it off for a few more minutes effectively trains him to listen to you.

To be effective, timeout must be administered immediately and without fuss. If it takes six aides to put a boy in a timeout room or if mother and father yell at each other and accuse each other of not handling their son correctly, the child may be getting the attention he wants anyway.

An adjunct to timeout is *response cost*. Especially in a token economy, points or tokens taken off for misbehavior has been shown to be extremely effective.

In dealing with extinction, timeout, and response cost, one must be aware of a great caution; aides, teachers and parents always find it easier to take things away. It is unfair for those children who have previously had little and who earn something only to have it removed. The logical outcome of continually taking away things is to have the child realize this, and that for everything he does, he may lose something he values and he will soon not try anything new. On the other hand, through positive reinforcement there are always new and wonderful things to work towards. The only negative outcome of positive reinforcement may be spoiling the child; spoiling does not often occur if the manipulation is handled correctly, and, in any case, is a small price to pay in having a child behave well.

RULES IN APPLYING PUNISHMENT

Most of the rules that apply to reinforcement also apply to punishment. The target behavior must be pinpointed; baseline data must be collected and charted; programs must be evaluated and/or modified, depending on the results. Punishment is only effective if the target behavior is weakened. Like reinforcement, punishment is most effective when it is immediate and given in greater quantities; the effects last longer when it is intermittent. Also the effects of punishment can be extinguished—when punishment is removed the punished behavior returns if other conditions remain the same. All these rules apply to both punishment and reinforcement.

SIDE EFFECTS IN THE USE OF PUNISHMENT

Punishment is not the preferred means of behavioral control because of the side effects that usually accompany its use.

1. Especially with physical punishment, the use of punishment often causes the child to *avoid* or *escape* from the person who punishes. Thus the child might learn to cheat, run away, lie, hide, or sneak in order to avoid punishment or to escape from the punisher.

2. When the parent uses physical punishment, the child is provided with a *model of aggression,* since children often imitate what they see their parents doing.

3. In addition, since punishment often produces an emotional scene which is unpleasant for the parent as well as the child, the methods might not be used consistently by the parent and the be-

havior would be unsystematically controlled and not decrease.

Although punishment weakens maladaptive behaviors, used alone it does not provide adaptive behaviors to take their place. You might stop a child from fighting by taking away five cents from his allowance each time he fights, but you are not teaching him how to interact properly with his friends. For this reason, programs that use punishment to weaken an inappropriate behavior should also include reinforcement to improve a competing appropriate behavior.

(*Caution:* Use reinforcement whenever possible before using punishment. Where punishment is necessary, use extinction or timeout.)

To use punishment effectively it is important to keep in mind certain principles. The withdrawal of reinforcers is most effective in weakening maladaptive behavior when the child is also provided with a way to earn the reinforcers back. The child stays quietly in his room for three minutes; he may then come out of his room and receive attention. Or he can have his dish back if he eats properly with a spoon. This method somewhat prevents avoidance and escape behaviors from being learned—the child recovers the reinforcer when he behaves appropriately and no great fear or hate need be involved. To reduce the chances that the child learns to hate and fear the punisher, appropriate behaviors should also be reinforced as part of the program in which punishment is being used. The child then learns that he is still loved even though he has to be punished for certain behaviors. If possible, physical punishment should be avoided, since hate is developed more easily if you physically hurt someone. Also, it is important to be calm and not act angry when you are punishing, since anger also might increase feelings of hate. To make punishment most effective it is also useful to have a *warning signal* before punishing. Soon the warning signal alone should be sufficient to stop a behavior. Thus, if every time the child has a tantrum he is told "stop that" and is then put in his room for three minutes, the warning signal "stop that" should eventually become a *learned punisher* and be enough to stop the behavior. The child will anticipate that the punishment is coming. In the same manner, saying "no" or "don't" before punishing makes these words effective learned punishers and more severe punishment will no longer become necessary.

As was mentioned previously, behaviors which are not compatible with a child's inappropriate behaviors should be reinforced so that punishment is needed less often. In this way the child is provided with appropriate ways to get attention or other reinforcement. Also, as in all behavioral control, *consistency* is very important—it is much more difficult to weaken a behavior that is sometimes punished and sometimes reinforced. The following cases illustrate some of the above principles of punishment.

CASE 1

Mike is a twelve-year-old, moderately-retarded child who lives at home. His mother is concerned because he uses his fingers to eat out of his plate and the plates of others, although he knows how to use eating utensils properly and knows good table manners. The mother collected baseline data for each meal for six days.

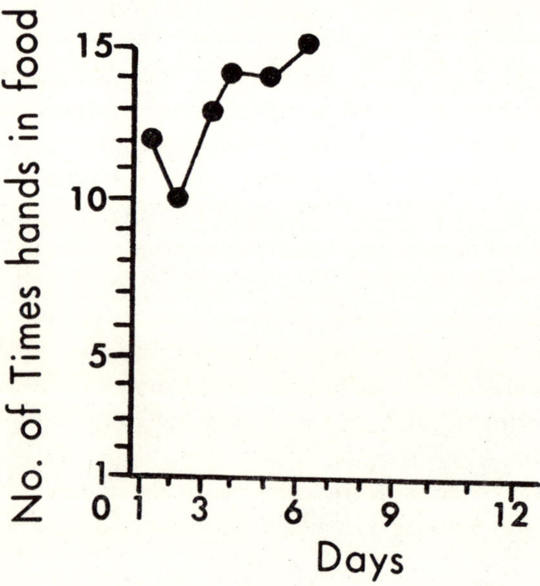

Figure 12.

On the seventh day a program was initiated whereby:

1. The first time Mike put his hands in his food he was told "No—eat with your fork."

2. The second time that he put his hands in his food, and each time thereafter, he was told "No—eat with your fork" and his plate was taken away for approximately thirty seconds. Then his plate was given back.

3. If he ate with a fork when the plate was returned, he was praised.

4. If he had a meal during which he did not put his hands in food, he got a star on a chart and a lot of social praise. The star entitled him to have his father read him a story after dinner.

After one week the data were as follows:

Mike's Progress

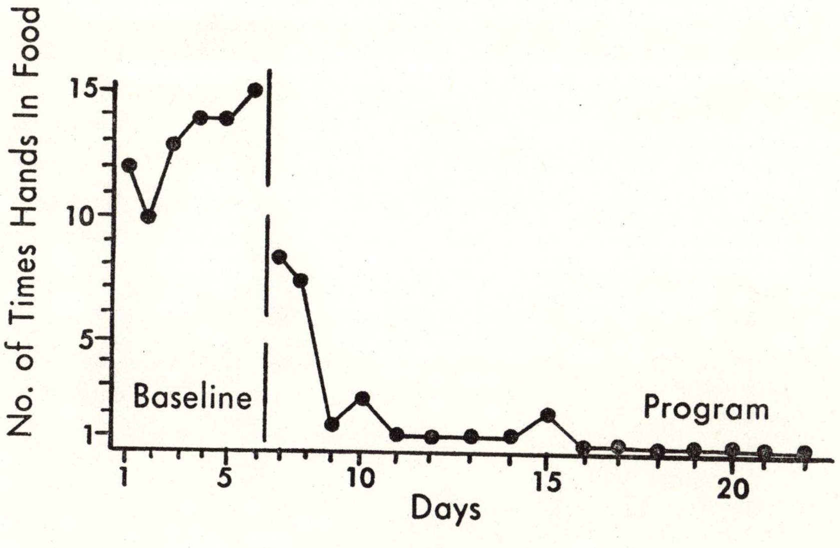

Figure 13.

This program had all the components of effective use of punishment.

1. No physical punishment was used; withdrawal of something good (the food) was used as a punisher.

2. He had a way to earn back and keep the reinforcer that is, by losing the food for thirty seconds, and when it was returned, by not putting his hands into the food.

3. No anger was exhibited by mother. She calmly said, "No, eat with your fork," and the plate was removed for thirty seconds.

4. An appropriate behavior was also being reinforced—using proper eating utensils.

5. A warning signal was used "No, eat with your fork."

6. The family was consistent in following through with both punishment and rewards.

CASE 2

Marsha is a six-year-old girl with an older brother, Jerry, who is ten years old. The mother complained that Marsha would take her brother's toys and either hide them or break them, thus provoking fights with her brother. Since her brother was stronger, she usually ended up getting hurt; Marsha was then given sympathy while her brother was scolded. The mother knew that this was wrong but could not think of

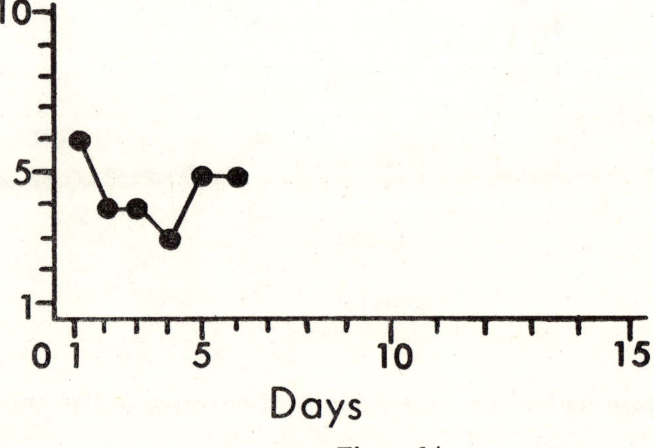

Figure 14.

any way to change things. The mother was asked to collect data on the target behavior of the number of toys Marsha takes from her brother. Mother checked Marsha's room before each meal and asked Jerry if any of his toys were missing to get an accurate count.

It was felt that part of the reason that Marsha took Jerry's things was that he never paid attention to her. A program was set up to use Jerry's attention as a reinforcer for not taking his toys; Marsha was also to be punished for taking toys. Mother made a chart on which she put a check mark for each toy Marsha took from Jerry. Every evening after dinner Marsha, Jerry, and both parents would have an activity together for thirty minutes, either playing ball outside, singing songs around the piano, or working on an arts and crafts project. For each check mark on her chart Marsha lost ten minutes time with the family. While the group was together, cooperation between the two children was reinforced. Furthermore, rather than yell or fight with his sister, Jerry could tell mother what was missing which he was rewarded for as being a "helper." Also, both Jerry and Marsha were given their own box in which they could keep their toys.

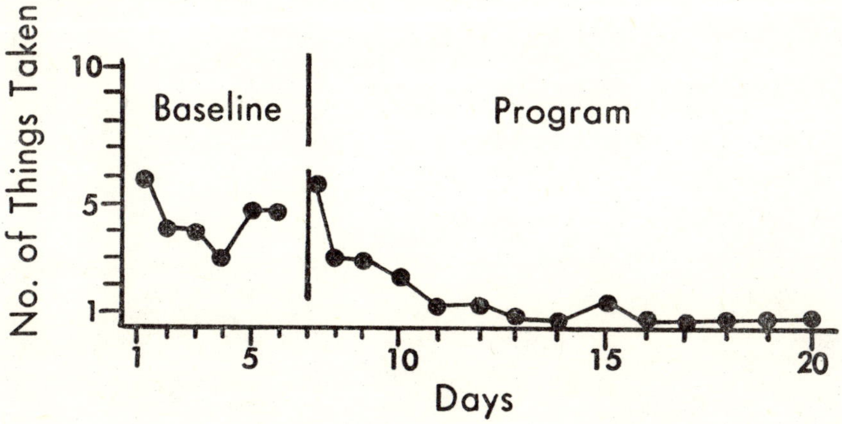

Figure 15.

HOME ASSIGNMENT

1. For each problem behavior of your child, list several incompatible behaviors which he could do instead of the problem behavior.

2. Practice administering punishment by yourself (removal of desirable things *not* a slap) matter-of-factly, in your room or before a mirror.

3. How could you implement extinction and timeout in your home, in your car, at dinner, at a friend's home? (give examples of each)

CHAPTER IX

PARENT AS TRAINER: EXAMPLES OF PARENTS USING BEHAVIOR MODIFICATION TECHNIQUES

EACH OF THE FOLLOWING EXAMPLES of programs was designed and implemented by mothers who attended an eight-week course in how to deal with their child's problem behaviors using behavior modification techniques. At the weekly meetings, the parents were given chapters of this book; contact between the trainer and the parents was kept through a telephone call every second day. The following examples are given to show that parents can be effective trainers.

CASE A

Description

Caucasian male, five years of age of middle-class family. Older sister six years of age. Mother came to the Neuropsychiatric Institute requesting aid in dealing with "A". Presenting complaints were that the child had no friends; parents of other children would not allow them to play with "A" because he was so aggressive. The boy would not be separated from his mother and fussed when he was dropped at the nursery school. He was disruptive in school and the teacher raised the question of mental retardation and whether or not he would be ready for kindergarten and school. This prompted the mother to bring him to NPI.

Both mother and son were seen by a team. "A" would not separate from his mother, would not raise his eyes, spoke unintelligibly, and would not allow himself to be held. Testing indicated a borderline level of intelligence, but much of his poor performance could be related to his lack of responsiveness. On the Vineland Social Maturity Scale he scored at a three-year old level. The mother was tired-looking and depressed. She said very little and kept her eyes downcast.

The recommendation was that the mother begin in a parent

training group and that the son would be seen by a psychology trainee for preacademic training.

Parent Questionnaire Before Training

1. What is your major problem with your child?

His behavior, especially outside the home. He has a very difficult time relating to anyone except me. Even his father sometimes asks me what he is saying. If strangers are around, he just puts down his head and ignores them. He won't answer if asked a question. In stores he is a terror. He'll run off to the toy department as soon as we get in the store. If I hold his hand he goes limp and I have to drag or carry him. If I spank him, he screams so loud I draw a crowd.

2. What does he do exactly (behavioral definition)?

He does an enormous amount of "nonsense talking." He will go on with this until we're ready to scream! He'll often do it when there is a conversation already going on. He can't participate, so he does his own talking about his own topic; even I don't understand him then. He just talks about nothing. He also asks me "nonsense questions" in a high-pitched tone. He keeps poking me and asking questions over and over. It's very annoying. With his "friends" he also has problems. If there's more than one playing, it always ends in a fight. If there's just one, they'll play until the friend has had his fill of Tommy and leaves.

3. When does the "nonsense talking" occur?

I've noticed A's "nonsense talking" occurs more outside the home. He does it quite often in the car; his mind seems to wander and before you know it he's on his way. He does it, too, in front of strangers. Many times he'll do it if asked a question. Sometimes I don't know if he's playing a game with me, or if he's just saying anything in order to give an answer.

4. How often does the "nonsense talking" happen? How long does it last?

When A is around other children he does it quite often. He seems to deliberately antagonize them until they hit him or remove him bodily. He "nonsense talks" anytime we're in a new or strange place, he gets very excited and does it until we get home.

5. What happens to him after he does it? What do you do? What does father do? What do siblings do? Others?

When A misbehaves in the store I usually end up taking him behind a counter and giving him a spanking. He screams *so* loud people turn around from the other side of the store. When A gets in trouble with his friends, I usually bring him in to stop the fight. A's father has no trouble with him in the store and when his father is home he seldom gets into fights with neighborhood children. His sister can't stand him around her friends. Her friends run away from him.

6. Does anything seem to affect the "nonsense talk" behavior? Anything you or anyone else does?

As I said before, it's outside of the home that A turns into the terror. Also at home when there is company, he acts extremely immature. His father, however, has very little problem with him. He is a very strict disciplinarian. A just stays out of his way.

7. How is he usually rewarded? For what is he rewarded?

Sometimes he is rewarded with an ice cream cone. But the more I think about it the more I realize I'm rewarding him for being naughty. You see, he's naughty but I've already told him if he were good he would get it and I hate to start trouble. His father takes the children for pony rides. They adore this. I guess I don't praise him enough. I think it's because I don't know if he's capable of much more and is just putting me on.

8. How is he usually punished? For what is he punished? How does he react?

My husband punishes A with spankings and scoldings and by sending him to his room. I don't punish him much. I yell a lot but I think he knows he can get away with things. Sometimes he's punished for going into neighbor's garages and taking their tools or taking his father's tools out. He might get into my make-up or maybe he'll leave the house and go on the street. He takes punishment quite well. He'll cry for a while, then apologize.

9. What are some other problem behaviors that he exhibits?

He picks his nose quite frequently.
He walks on his toes very often.
He makes up a grace of his own saying "stupid God."
He says he "hates" to everyone and about everyone.
He talks in a high-pitched voice.

10. Being the mother of this child makes me feel . . .

Pre-Training

. . . filled with many many emotions. I'm sure all mothers have some mixed feelings about their children, no matter how *normal* they are. When he accomplishes something new and relatively difficult for him, I am as proud as any mother would be seeing her child progressing. In fact, my feelings are probably a lot stronger because I realize the effort that was put forth.

The sadness I feel because of A's handicap is extremely deep. I feel very disappointed, mostly in myself. I was the only one in a family of seven who didn't complete college. I have done nothing with my life. I couldn't even have children successfully. I was never very athletic; my brothers and sisters were. My body was always frail. I begged for anesthetic when I was delivering and I got it. I'm sure that because of that I couldn't "help" to get Tommy out of the birth canal.

At times I am angry. Angry with God for giving me a less than perfect child. Angry with the looks people give A. Even angry with A because I cannot control him.

A and I have a wonderful love for each other. He brings me an enormous amount of happiness. I am very hopeful that A can be helped.

Post-Training

It still wears me out. Sometimes I think that it sure would've been a lot easier if I never had him, or my daughter for that matter. But the change has been fantastic. He is not the same little boy I brought to you a few short months ago; and I'm not the same mother either. I am really happy. I don't feel guilty when I have to punish him. I don't *yell* either. I try *not* to get into power struggles. I change antecedents all over the place and I've become a master at "structural engineering" with my whole family. I always go around a problem rather than meeting it head on.

I am really very grateful. *Thank you all!*

Training Case A's Mother

Class 1

Counting is discussed. Frequency and rate counting are both discussed. Parents select one target behavior and count that for a week. This mother counted the number of times the boy talked inappropriately which was defined as interjecting into conversations or speaking peculiarly (e.g. "where's the house?") .

Telephone Call (two days later)

Mother is having success counting. She feels structured, more organized.

Class 2

Graphed data (given introduction to reinforcement). A's mother feels much more confident about controlling children. Her physical appearance has improved.

Home Visit

Daughter and son friendly. The boy ignores questions, speaks slowly and unintelligibly—both the girl and his mother interpret for him. His sister and he argue; she teases him. His sister says she hates him. The boy continually uses negativistic speech; he hates sister, toys, school, etc.

Mother scolds both children, but is not obeyed, primarily because mother does not follow through. For example, at mealtime, grace is to be said before eating. The boy began eating while Mother said, "stop it," four times, and the child continued eating. Mother responds quickly to children's requests for aid even though both can perform the task (clothing selves).

Class 3

(Discussion of reinforcement principles and establishment of program for improving behavior.) Mother has been ignoring nonsense talking and feels that it is decreasing. She feels more confident. She has very good questions about *Parent Training Manual*. She is using terminology even though we do not stress it. She brings coffee pot, coffee and cups for entire group.

Class 4

(Continued monitoring of behavior; program evaluated and changed; punishment discussed.) Mother has begun reinforcing "speaking well" by the boy and continues ignoring "nonsense talking." In addition, she has been trained in working with the boy on matching colors and concepts to improve his chances of being allowed into kindergarten. Nonsense talking drops right down. He is speaking more carefully and clearly. He will look up and be held by stranger. He is not afraid of being kept from Mother.

Class 5

(New program devised.) Mother is emphasizing preacademic training skills now. A can match colors. He uses concepts large-small three dimensionally, as well as big-little, round-not round. We are now working on same-different. He names colors. He responds well to candy reinforcement.

Father is taking interest in the boy; this is the best reinforcer of all. Father's bragging about son's progress reinforces his mother.

Class 6

(Generalization discussed.) Progress continues well. A is accepted in nursery placement; Mother can work in the nursery as well. Mother enjoys this. Daughter is also improved; petty jealousies have stopped now that Mother divides time equally between son and daughter.

Results

Figure 16 is a graphic display of A's "nonsense talking" during baseline and extinction. When the mother began ignoring "nonsense talking," the rate dropped and was extinguished when the mother walked out of the room or away from the child, thereby eliminating the secondary reinforcement value of the mother. A's "hate talk" was also ignored while reinforcement for appropriate language was given so the former extinguished and the latter increased significantly. The psychology trainee worked individually, weekly, for an hour with the boy while his mother observed how to obtain and maintain the boy's attention for training on preacademic skills. Videotapes were used as well. The mother carried on the academic training at home.

Academically, after two months, the boy performed hourly sessions without tiring. His attention and speech were quickly brought under control and improved. He learned basic colors, some concepts, and began using books. He made so much progress that he was admitted into a cooperative nursery school where the mother could work with him. The mother was no longer afraid to take him to stores and he has maintained friends. His Vineland Social Maturity Scale level was now four years, seven months.

The mother's attitude changed so drastically that when it came time to complete the questionnaire again, she responded by saying that she no longer had a problem. The boy is now considered to have an excellent basis for kindergarten and first grade. Generalization of mother's training has carried over to the daughter.

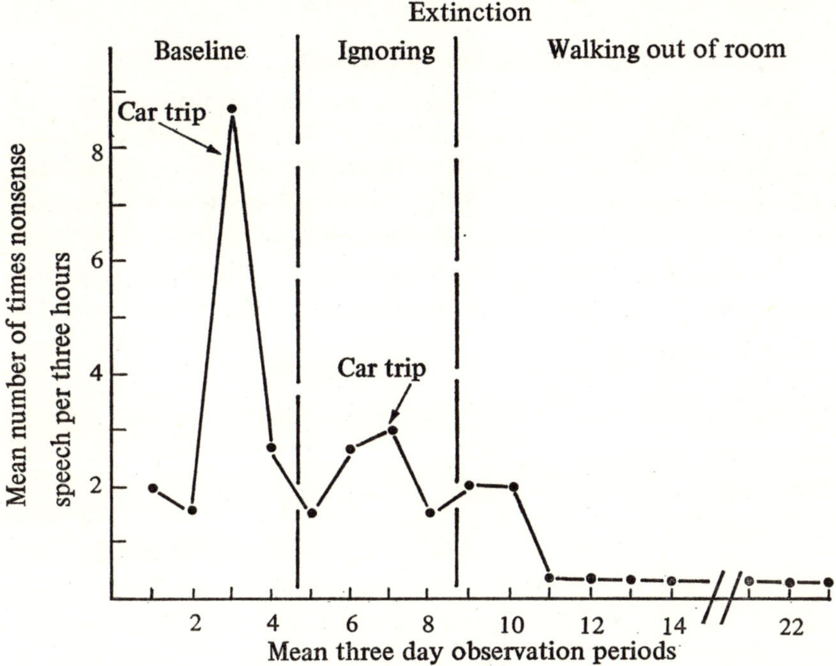

Figure 16.

CASE B

Extinguishing Hitting Baby

A seven year eight month, moderately-retarded female of an intact middle class family with an infant sibling as well as an older brother. She was attending a school for the retarded, but her behavior problems both at school and at home forced her mother to seek help. At school, the child's problems were pulling her hair, hyperactivity, and temper tantrums. At home, the child's temper tantrums (biting herself, pulling things from drawers) and fits of jealousy (hitting the baby) had reached a point where, in the latter case, the mother was afraid of the baby's being hurt.

On the home visit, it was seen that temper tantrums and the hurting of the baby were related. It also appeared that the mother was attempting to apply some training methods that she was learning as part of another program, but that she was extremely inconsistent. The child has little speech, but the mother interprets for her, lifts her up to select food, dresses her, and allows her to eat with her fingers.

Program and Results

The mother was enrolled in the parent training group with "hitting the baby" as the target behavior. The rate of this behavior was observed for two weeks as a baseline, since training sessions were weekly and it was not until the second week that extinction was introduced. Figure 17 contains depiction of the rate.

The program initiated was to tell the child that she would be removed from the room where the baby was if she hit or pushed or

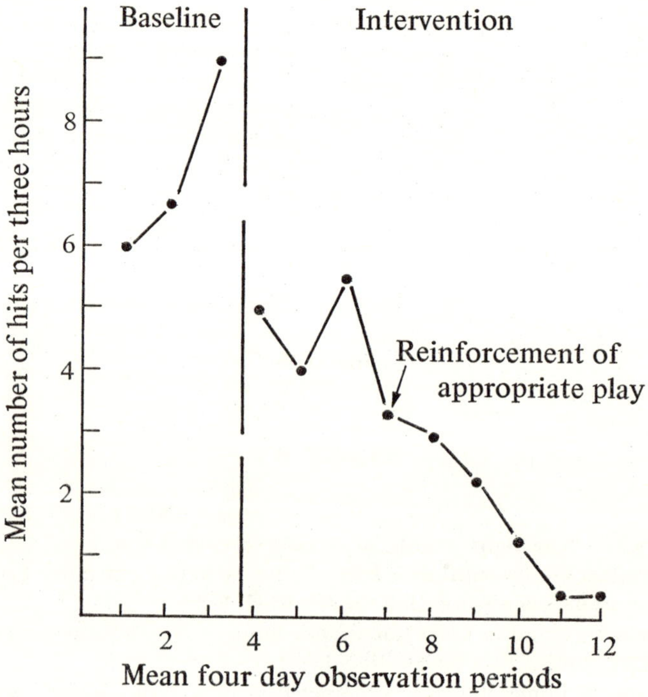

Figure 17.

pulled or put paper in the baby's mouth, etc. The rate dropped, but fluctuated. When reinforcement was introduced into class, the mother began reinforcing appropriate play with the baby as well as removal of the child from the baby for two minutes timed on a timer. The mother supervised two to ten-minute periods of interacting with the baby where the child held the baby, pushed him in the carriage, showed him a doll or rattle, and talked to him. If there was any inappropriate action, the baby was picked up by the mother and taken away. The mother considered the program to be successful.

CASE C

A Compulsive Eater

Charlene was a cute, six-year-old mildly-retarded girl who constantly raided the refrigerator. She was capable of understanding the terms of a behavioral contract; however, her sister demanded to be treated in the same manner. The two following behavior contracts listed in Table XXIV were posted. Charlene was given a token for each fifteen minutes that she did not go to the refrigerator, and Andrea was given a token for each fifteen minutes of appropriate play, and both had to pay for their rewards according to the established costs.

TABLE XXIX.
BEHAVIORAL CONTRACT COSTS

	Charlene		*Andrea*
1	Watch TV	1	Watch TV
1	Read stories to Dad	1	Read stories to Dad
1	Have Dad read stories	5	Buy candy (10c)
		5	Eat in cafeteria
5	Eat in cafeteria	10	Swim at Tanya's
5	Paint pictures with Dad	10	Horseback riding
10	Pony riding	25	Beverly Glen Park
25	Beverly Glen Park	25	"fancy" restaurants (Andre's)
50	Disneyland	50	Disneyland
50	Japanese Village	50	Japanese Village
50	Magic Mountain	50	Magic Mountain
50	New toys ($2.00)	50	New toys ($2.00)

Figure 18 contains Charlene's progress.

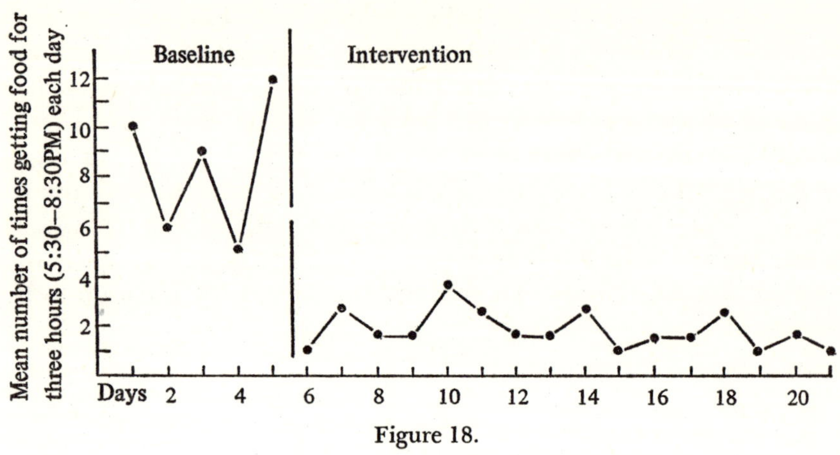

Figure 18.

CASE D

Hyperactive-Behavior Problem Boy

David was a behavior problem both at home and at school. He always refused to get up on time, take his medication, to dress and to shower unless the mother repeatedly reminded him. The mother contacted the teacher and asked her to use a simple five-item checklist (on time to school, no warnings, completed reading, completed arithmetic, and completed spelling) which the teacher would fill out for David to be taken home for token reinforcement. Praise and stars at school would also be given. As a result of this combined program, David's school problems diminished and he completed his academic work.

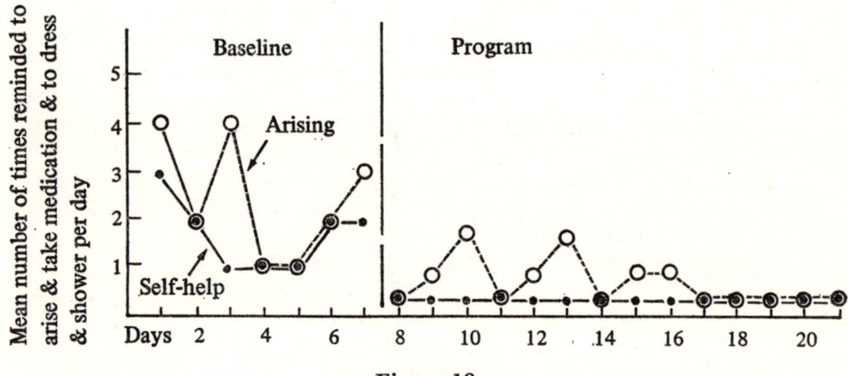

Figure 19.

CASE E

Toilet Training a Normal Two-year-Old Girl

Nancy's mother attended a group to learn more about normal development and decided to work on toilet training. She complimented Nancy each time Nancy either said she had to go to the potty (urination only) or went herself. Figure 20 shows Nancy's progress. After the introduction of reinforcement Nancy had no accidents in the house, and at the time the mother left the group accidents outside the home had almost disappeared.

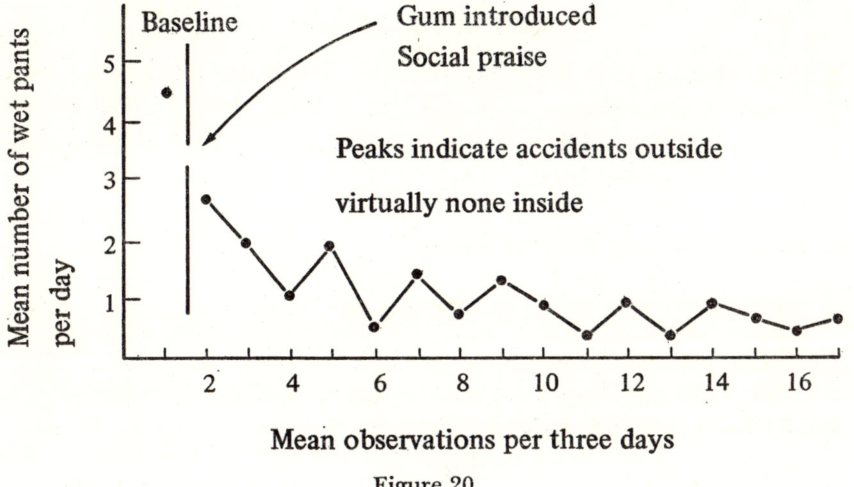

Figure 20.

CHAPTER X

PROBLEMS IN MAKING PROGRAMS WORK; SOME CAUTIONS

Lack of Consistency

USUALLY PARENTS have been doing something for so long that they cannot change and may ruin a program's effectiveness by being inconsistent. Often parents will set rules and allow themselves to be coerced by the child to break them. Consistency is the most important aspect of any program; the child knows what he must do and so also does the parent.

Initial Success

When a parent who previously has not really paid attention to a child suddenly begins observing and counting and writing a child's behaviors on a sheet of paper, the problem behavior may suddenly disappear. Parents think that this has corrected the problem and may cease listening to a trainer or reading what to do next or being consistent in recording. Unfortunately, these parents are deluding themselves; since the parents' behavior has changed a little, so has that of their child. The child wonders about this change, but will soon become used to it and he will become his old problem self again.

Lack of Reinforcement for the Parent

Often parents complain that they are doing all of this work and are not getting any rewards for it. Rewards come to parents in many ways. One of the best is through the satisfaction of seeing their own child improve. By using graphs, the parent can see even the smallest improvement. Another way is by hearing of the child's improvement from teachers, relatives or the spouse. Another is from feeling effective as a parent, by a feeling of competency. Unfortunately, praising does not seem to come easy to many people. For this reason, the spouse should be involved as well, so that he is aware of all the work that his spouse is undertaking. An excellent example of how much a spouse's praise means, however indirect, occurred with the mother of Case A (described in the last chapter). The mother had not received any praise for being an adequate mother and had even been criticized by the husband for inadequacy. Once the program had started to succeed, and the father was forced to recognize the success because the change in the boy's behavior was so great, he mentioned at a dinner party how marvelous the program was that *they* were doing with the boy. Although the father had done little, the mother was overwhelmed by his indirect compliment and by the subsequent attention by the dinner guests, so much so, in fact, that she telephoned the trainer to convey her gratification.

Trainers should also be aware of their roles as reinforcers for parent trainers. Having an assistant call the parent once or twice a week can do much to reinforce her continuation of her work.

Sabotaging by Siblings or Spouse

Older siblings may sabotage a parent's program for training a child, either wittingly or unwittingly. The sibling may openly encourage the child to disobey rules; the child may model after the older child's freedom to do what he wishes or the older child may surrepticiously give the sibling candies or money.

One way out of this dilemma is to make all of the older children aware of the parent's program. These children can also be reinforced for observing the rules of the program. Or alternately, these children could be trained themselves to work with the problem child. Care must be taken to insure that the older children do not misuse their control over the child and subjugate him.

BIBLIOGRAPHY

Axelrod, S.: Token reinforcement programs in special classes. *Except Child,* January, 371-379, 1971.

Becker, W.: *Parents Are Teachers.* Champaign, Res Press, 1971.

Bensberg, G.: *Teaching the Mentally Retarded.* Atlanta, Southern Regional Education Board, 1965.

Buckley, N., and Walker, H.: *Modifying Classroom Behavior: A Manual of Procedure for Classroom Teachers.* Champaign, Res Press, 1970.

Kuypers, D., Becker, N., and O'Leary, K.: How to make a token system fail. *Except Child, 35*:101-109, 1968.

Lovass, O.: Establishment of speech in psychotic children. In Sloane, Jr., H., and Mac Aulay, B. (Eds.): *Operant Procedure in Remedial Speech and Language Training.* New York, H-M, 1968.

McKenzie, H., Clark, M., Wolf, M., Kotherd, R., and Benson, C.: Behavior modification of children with learning disabilities using grades as tokens and allowances as back-up reinforcers. *Except Child, 34*:745-752, 1968.

Patterson, G.: *Families: Application of Social Learning to Family Life.* Champaign, Res Press, 1971.

Patterson, G., and Gullion, M.: *Living with Children.* Champaign, Res Press, 1968.

Thorndike, E.: *Animal intelligence.* New York: Macmillan, 1911.

Thorndike, E.: *The psychology of learning.* New York: Teachers College, 1913.

Ullman, L., and Krasner, L.: *Case Studies in Behavior Modification.* New York, H R & W, 1965.

APPENDICES

APPENDIX I

SUMMARY OF CAUTIONS

CAUTION I: Take into consideration a child's stage of development before assuming that *either* his behavior is abnormal *or* that he can do a particular task that you require of him.

CAUTION II: In defining and counting how often a behavior occurs, make sure that the behavior is objective, that is one which other people could also count.

CAUTION III: In counting how often a behavior occurs, make sure that there is a stable rate of occurrence and not extreme swings.

CAUTION IV: Use positive reinforcement whenever you can.

CAUTION V: Restructure the environment before attempting any program to make sure that the behavior is not a transitory phenomenon.

CAUTION VI: Change reinforcers if a child appears to be satiated by a single reinforcer.

CAUTION VII: Use secondary reinforcers whenever possible and try to establish enjoyment in doing the task.

CAUTION VIII: *Be consistent* in all of your programs. Change contingencies only after you see demonstrable changes in your records (graphs).

CAUTION IX: If punishment must be used, use extinction or timeout and not the administration of a punisher (e.g. slap).

CAUTION X: Use a Warning Signal (verbal command) whenever possible.

APPENDIX II

OUTLINE OF PROGRAM FOR ELIMINATING PROBLEM BEHAVIOR

1. Define problem behavior.
2. Define behavior incompatible to problem behavior.
3. Count (frequency, time or rate) baseline occurrence of problem behavior.
4. Record (graph) results of counting.
5. List reinforcers for child (positive and negative).
6. Look at environment and restructure if necessary to change occurrence of behavior.
7. Set, list and explain rules to child (what he must do and how often, to get what).
8. Shape behavior.
9. Continue recording.
10. Implement extinction, timeout or response cost if reinforcement of incompatible behavior does not work.
11. Raise criterion for reinforcement.
12. Reinforce intermittently.
13. Wean from tangible reinforcers.
14. Go on to another behavior.
15. Continue recording.
16. *Optional:* Reversal and reinstatement of contingencies.

OUTLINE OF PROGRAM FOR IMPLEMENTING AND STRENGTHENING ADAPTIVE BEHAVIOR

1. Specify adaptive behavior.
2. Break down behavior into smallest parts.
3. Determine at what stage child performs.
4. Structure a favorable situation for training.
5. List and establish reinforcers for performance.

6. Institute beginnings of desired response.

7. Successively shape performance using continual reinforcement.

8. Continue recording.

9. Remove prompting.

10. Reinforce intermittently.

APPENDIX III

QUESTIONS

THESE QUESTIONS ARE to be used with the material in the book. They are arranged in topic categories of classical and operant conditioning; measurement; types of reinforcement; reinforcement effect; schedules of reinforcement; and in shaping and ways to decrease maladaptive behavior. Within topics, there are both multiple choice and true-false questions and there are several stories with fill-in-the-blank paragraphs. Answers to all questions are listed at the very end.

CLASSICAL VERSUS OPERANT CONDITIONING

1. Pairing a verbal command with ice cream noncontingently on the response of the child is called
   a. classical conditioning. b. operant conditioning. c. instrumental conditioning.
2. Contingent means
   a. next to. b. because of. c. dependent upon. d. after.
3. The "law of effect" states that
   a. what you do has an effect on other people.
   b. every cause has an effect.
   c. consequences of an action will increase or decrease the probability of that action occurring again.
4. The law of effect was stated by
   a. Skinner. b. Thorndike. c. Pavlov. d. Watson.
5. Which of the following is *not* a rule for using positive reinforcement?
   a. The effectiveness of a reinforcer depends upon its magnitude.
   b. Allow the child to sample the reinforcer ahead of time (i.e. being familiar with the reinforcer).
   c. The kind of reinforcer used.

    d. A reinforcer should be used on a simple behavior.

    e. None of the above.

6. Which of the following statements is most true?

    a. Behavior is not learned.

    b. Only inappropriate behaviors are learned.

    c. Both inappropriate and appropriate behaviors are learned.

    d. Almost all behaviors are learned.

7. Which of the following statements is true about the trainer (i.e. parent, teacher, etc.) ?

    a. He possesses full control over the situation (i.e. interaction).

    b. His behavior is never affected by the child.

    c. He is liable to the same principles of behavior modification covertly as he is applying overtly to the child.

8. The examples of the dog phobia and the school phobia were most effectively treated by the process of

    a. immediately pairing the feared object with a pleasant stimulus.

    b. removing the feared object contingent upon a nonfearful response.

    c. pairing a pleasant stimulus while bringing closer a feared object or bringing the subject closer to the feared object.

9. The reason why operant conditioning techniques have been used more often than classical conditioning techniques with the mentally retarded and developmentally disabled is

    a. because classical conditioning is a more effective procedure.

    b. because classical conditioning only emphasizes removal of behavior without an equal emphasis upon building more adaptive behaviors.

    c. This is not a true statement; classical conditioning is just as effective as operant conditioning.

Check True or False on the following:

10. Behavior modification can only work with behaviors present in the repertoire of the person.

    T   F

11. Very often a problem child acts the way he does not because of some intrinsic problem but because he has learned to act this way.

    T   F

12. Skinner found that only pigeons could be taught new behaviors.
    T   F
13. Behavior modification techniques only apply when dealing with behaviors, not academic skills.
    T   F
14. Appropriate and inappropriate behaviors are so defined because of some intrinsic property of the behavior.
    T   F
15. Systematic desensitization is a form of operant conditioning.
    T   F
16. Phobias or fears are best treated by classical conditioning.
    T   F
17. In operant conditioning the response is affected by its consequences, whereas in classical conditioning the consequences bear no impact on the occurrence of the behavior.
    T   F

MEASUREMENT

1. Evidence suggesting that special class teachers spend 70 percent of their time attending to nonacademic behaviors and 30 percent of their time attending to academic behaviors was gathered by
   a. time sampling technique.
   b. duration measure of attention.
   c. rating scales.
   d. two of the above.
2. In defining adaptive behaviors it is imperative
   a. to make sure the behavior is within the child's developmental abilities.
   b. to make sure that operant techniques can be applied to the behavior.
   c. to make sure that the behavior does not conflict with any past anxieties.
3. An example of a good "operational definition" for Joey's tantrum would be
   a. running up and down a hall 3 x 15 screaming.
   b. giving mother a hard time at dinner and being very resistant.

   c. incidence of screaming, crying or physically attacking a person or objects, whenever it occurs and for however long it lasts.

   d. none of these.

4. To obtain an objective record of how strong a behavior is and how frequently it occurs it is necessary to systematically
   a. count the behavior.
   b. chart the behavior over time.
   c. graph the behavior over time.
   d. all of the above.

5. Response strength can be estimated by
   a. the amount of reinforcement.
   b. rate of response, magnitude of response, latency of response.
   c. resistance to extinction.
   d. all of the above.
   e. b and c.

6. The advantage of taking a baseline measure
   a. is to permit you to notice small improvements in the behavior that might otherwise go unnoticed.
   b. is to gain extra experience with the behavior to be measured.
   c. occurs only when we are running an experiment in the laboratory.
   d. none of the above.

7. Taking baseline on a behavior refers to that aspect of determining the behavior which entails
   a. graphing and charting the behavior over time.
   b. defining the problem behavior to be measured.
   c. measuring the behavior in an attempt to ascertain the strength of the behavior previous to the institution of an intervention program.
   d. determining the rate of the behavior.

8. When Joey throws his tantrums they usually last one to two hours and occur once or twice a day. The best way to measure this tantrum behavior is to determine
   a. rate of tantrums.
   b. frequency of tantrums.
   c. duration of tantrums.

    d. latency.
9. It is necessary to define and measure a behavior that you want to work on in order to
    a. determine response strength.
    b. determine an effective intervention program.
    c. develop an objective perception of the problem if indeed it is found to be a problem.
    d. two of the above.
    e. all of the above.

Check True or False to the following:

10. The first step towards an intervention program are to (a) define the problem behavior. (b) define the adaptive behavior and (c) count the problem behavior.
    T   F

11. As long as you have recorded the strength of a behavior before starting your intervention program you need not concern yourself with antecedent events or consequences of the behavior.
    T   F

12. The *rate* of a behavior is the frequency of the behavior divided by the latency of the behavior.
    T   F

TYPES OF REINFORCEMENT

1. Joey enjoys eating at the dinner table with his parents and friends; when he does not eat properly they make him eat alone in the kitchen.
    a. Joey has been negatively punished.
    b. Joey is in timeout.
    c. Joey has been negatively reinforced.
    d. Both b and c.
    e. Both a and b.

2. The social reinforcing properties of a stimulus are acquired
    a. by being paired with a tangible reinforcer.
    b. by being paired with other social reinforcers.
    c. as a result of contiguous presentation with some behavior.
    d. none of these.

3. Which of these statements is true?

   a. All children do not work equally well for the same reinforcer.

   b. A child does not work equally well all the time for the same reinforcer.

   c. Reinforcers must be individually established.

   d. All of the above.

4. Social reinforcement is

   a. a primary reinforcer.

   b. a secondary reinforcer.

   c. an acquired reinforcer.

   d. a conditioned reinforcer.

   e. a, b and c.

   f. b, c and d.

5. In operant conditioning the removal of an aversive stimulus serves as a

   a. positive reinforcer.

   b. neutral reinforcer.

   c. negative reinforcer.

   d. both a and c.

6. Depriving Joey of baseball practice until he cleans his room is an example of

   a. cost contingency.

   b. withdrawing an activity reinforcer.

   c. negative punishment.

   d. two of the above.

7. A primary reinforcement is something which

   a. has intrinsic properties and is not learned.

   b. is learned and has no intrinsic properties.

   c. precedes a secondary reinforcer.

   d. is two of the above.

8. A tangible reinforcer is

   a. a primary reinforcer. b. a secondary reinforcer. c. both a and b.

9. The best argument against people who say that token reinforcement is ineffective and "alienates" the child is

   a. token reinforcement is consistent with the theory of behavior modification which has been proven empirically to be sound.

   b. it works. We all work for money and children work during the semester for grades.

   c. it works simply because the token is a reinforcer.

Check True or False on the following:

10. One of the biggest complaints parents have about extrinsic motivators is that the child will become dependent on M & M's for the rest of his life.

   T   F

11. Everybody works for a symbolic reinforcer at sometime in their life.

   T   F

12. Verbal reprimands are to negative reinforcement as tokens are to positive reinforcement.

   T   F

13. In a normal child one can expect that a behavior once rewarded with a tangible reinforcer paired with a social reinforcer will with maturation be carried out because of intrinsic satisfaction.

   T   F

14. When you pair a primary reinforcer with a secondary reinforcer you are using classical conditioning techniques.

   T   F

REINFORCEMENT EFFECT

1. Joey's younger brother is always taking his toys away. Complaining to Mommy did not solve the problem so Joey started hitting his younger brother, who quickly stopped.

   a. The younger brother stopped because he was positively punished for grabbing the toys.

   b. Joey will continue to hit his brother because he was positively reinforced when his younger brother stopped grabbing his toys.

   c. Joey will continue to hit his brother because he was negatively reinforced when his younger brother stopped grabbing his toys.

   d. Both a and b.

   e. Both a and c.

2. Johnny is having a temper tantrum because he broke his toy.

His mother rushes over and makes a fuss for him to stop; she hugs him and kisses him. What could happen?

a. Johnny will have a great deal of affection for his mother who understands him and comforts him.

b. Johnny will accidentally be reinforced with attention (a positive reinforcer) and his tantrum behavior will increase.

c. There will be no effect on Johnny's behavior.

d. The tantrum will be extinguished.

3. Joey does not like to do his math problems and starts swearing when he gets confused. Joey is then sent to his room as a punishment for swearing. What may happen?

a. Joey will be negatively reinforced for swearing because he gets out of doing his math.

b. Joey will be negatively reinforced for not doing his math.

c. Joey's swearing will increase.

d. Joey has learned an escape behavior.

e. Three of the above.

4. Michael's work habits in the classroom are poor. This situation is distressing for the teacher. When the teacher yells at him he starts working. What may happen?

a. Michael may build up a tolerance to the teacher's yelling, causing the teacher to yell louder.

b. The teacher will be negatively reinforced for yelling because yelling makes Michael work.

c. The teacher will use yelling more and more often to get Michael to work.

d. All of the above.

5. Charles used to cry every night before going to bed, not wanting his parents to leave until he fell asleep. This problem behavior was successfully extinguished. When Charles' aunt came to babysit she responded to his crying by coming to his room and staying with him. Charles tantrums started up again due to

a. spontaneous recovery.

b. inadvertant reinforcement.

c. it is impossible from this story to tell why.

6. Operant behavior can be affected in the following ways—

a. by positive reinforcement which increases the frequency of the behavior.

  b. by negative reinforcement which increases the frequency of
     the behavior.
  c. by negative reinforcement which decreases the frequency of
     the behavior.
  d. a and b.
  e. a and c.
7. To strengthen a behavior you need to
  a. remove a positive reinforcer.
  b. present a positive reinforcer.
  c. terminate or remove an aversive situation (apply a nega-
     tive reinforcer).
  d. not apply a negative reinforcer.
  e. b and c.
  f. b and d.

Check True or False on the following

8. Joey was put in the corner for crying. You remove him when
   he is completely quiet. Removing him from the corner is called
   positive reinforcement.
   T   F
9. Qualifying one's praise (i.e. "Johnny, you did a good job, but
   you could have done better") does not seriously curtail one's
   effectiveness as a positive agent.
   T   F
10. The effectiveness of a reinforcer should be to strengthen a
    behavior.
    T   F
11. The "criticism trap" is when you constantly criticize your child
    instead of positively reinforcing him.
    T   F
12. Negative reinforcement and punishment are the same thing.
    T   F

SCHEDULES OF REINFORCEMENT

1. Joey was being reinforced for cleaning up his room; (gets
   twenty-five cents); however, while he was cleaning up he was
   also swearing. It was soon noticed that Joey's behavior of swearing was increasing as well as his behavior of cleaning up his
   room.

   a. Swearing is a means of self-reinforcement for Joey.

   b. Joey was inadvertantly reinforced for swearing concomitantly with the behavior of cleaning his room.

   c. Cleaning the room became a reinforcer for swearing.

2. Your baby cries when he is hungry; you have decided to extinguish his behavior by not feeding him when he cries.

   a. You should feed him immediately after he stops crying.

   b. You should wait a few minutes after he stops crying before feeding him.

   c. You should reinforce him immediately before the time when you know he will start crying for food.

   d. None of the above.

3. Intermittent reinforcement is very valuable because

   a. it makes a response more resistant to extinction.

   b. it permits the child to assume some responsibility.

   c. it relieves the trainer from being constantly present.

   d. all of the above.

4. If you say to your child, "Do this now and I will give you the candy when we get home," you are using

   a. noncontingent reinforcement.

   b. delayed reinforcement.

   c. delayed discrimination.

5. If you reinforce a child with candy for every response (i.e. every time he smiles) you are using

   a. a primary reinforcer.

   b. a continuous reinforcement schedule.

   c. immediate reinforcement.

   d. both a and b.

   e. both a and c.

Check True or False on the following:

6. Noncontingent reinforcement or punishment will not affect a behavior because it has not been associated with the behavior.

   T   F

7. You have just changed your schedule of reinforcement from continuous to intermittent, you will notice a drop in the acquisition curve corresponding to the change in schedule.

   T   F

8. If a child stops crying and you reinforce him *immediately* after he stops you are reinforcing him for stopping to cry.
   T   F

9. Continuous reinforcement will make a response more resistant to extinction than intermittent reinforcement.
   T   F

10. If a child emits a good behavior (i.e. says "Mama") and you reinforce him immediately after, you are reinforcing the verbalization "Mama."
    T   F

11. The experiment with the vegetative idiot demonstrated that positive reinforcement, noncontingent upon a behavior, will increase that behavior.
    T   F

SHAPING AND WAYS TO DECREASE MALADAPTIVE BEHAVIOR

1. Joey's father is verbally reprimanding him for some bad behavior, but at the same time he is laughing.
   a. Joey is getting mixed messages.
   b. Joey will have a problem discriminating whether his behavior is in fact good or bad.
   c. Joey's behavior will be weakened.
   d. Both a and c.
   e. Both a and b.

2. Timeout is
   a. a way to weaken behavior by removing all reinforcers (negative and positive).
   b. a way to weaken behavior by removing all positive reinforcers.
   c. a way to weaken behavior by removing all negative reinforcers.

3. Joey will swear in front of his father but not in front of his mother. His father usually laughs at his swearing while his mother makes a point to punish him for it. Joey has
   a. generalized between both parents.
   b. discriminated between both parents.
   c. been positively reinforced by his father's laughing.

d. a and c.

e. b and c.

4. If you are dealing with a retarded child and you want to teach him how to dress,

   a. you should teach him what "get dressed" means.

   b. you should break the behavior down into its component parts (i.e. shirt, pants) .

   c. you should reinforce him consistently for every new step.

   d. both a and c.

   e. both b and c.

5. The process of reinforcing successive approximations is called

   a. immediate reinforcement.

   b. shaping.

   c. partial reinforcement.

   d. schedule of reinforcement.

6. In the case of the mute, autistic little girl, giving her candy for grunts, then noises, then for small vocalizations represents a process called

   a. generalization.   c. discrimination.

   b. shaping.   d. extinction.

7. Joey is very messy and never cleans his room. You have decided that he must clean up his room before he can go out to play.

   a. There should be no exceptions.

   b. If Joey has a very good reason then you will make an exception.

   c. You should use this program intermittently; otherwise he will learn to dislike being around the house.

8. When the experimenter stopped giving milk to the vegetative idiot for lifting up his arm slightly, he was

   a. extinguishing the behavior of lifting the arm.

   b. shaping the behavior of lifting the arm.

   c. punishing the behavior of lifting the arm.

   d. none of the above.

9. When you are setting up an intervention program your schedule of reinforcement should

   a. go from continuous to intermittent.

   b. go from intermittent to continuous.

   c. use either continuous or partial and never change.

10. Joey has always been punished by being locked up in the cellar which has no windows. Years later he finds it very difficult to take an elevator or go to the movies. What has happened?
    a. Joey has generalized from the cellar to all rooms with no windows.
    b. Joey is exhibiting operant behavior.
    c. The contingencies are no longer present for Joey as an adult; therefore the behavior he is exhibiting has no relation to his childhood.

11. The ultimate goal with any behavior that you want to establish in a child is to
    a. have it generalize to other situations.
    b. have it occur with regularity in that environment.
    c. have it discriminate to other situations.

12. If you decide to restructure the environment to change maladaptive behavior, you are dealing with
    a. antecedent events.
    b. consequential events.
    c. events that occur concomittently with the behavior.

13. You can manipulate the environment to change behaviors by
    a. removing the child from the environment.
    b. removing distracting or upsetting objects from the environment.
    c. removing the significant antecedent event.
    d. all of the above.

Check True or False on the following:

14. When you extinguish a behavior, you are removing all positive reinforcers.
    T F

15. When you decide to use reinforcement or punishment to deal with a behavior you are only considering the consequences.
    T F

16. One of the most important aspects of making an intervention program successful is to be consistent in whatever you decide to do.
    T F

17. It is very important not to give a child too many messages at

once. You should wait until he can remember all of them.
T   F

18. To initiate a behavior modification program it is not important to look at the antecedents of a behavior or the consequences; all you are interested in is the problem behavior
itself.
T   F

19. If a teacher decides to use certain reinforcement contingencies
to toilet train your child in school, once he gets home you need
not use the same procedure.
T   F

20. If you set up a program to teach your child to clean up after
dinner and he starts by doing one thing (i.e. washing the
dishes) reinforcing dishwashing will eventually generalize to
cleaning the table and putting the dishes away.
T   F

APPLICATION OF THESE PRINCIPLES

Read the story first and then fill in the blanks of the accompany-
ing paragraphs using words from those listed below. This list is to
be used for all stories and words may sometimes be used more than
once.

frequency	behaviors
latency	aversive situation
duration	aversive stimulus
timeout	reinforcement
positive reinforcement	consequence (s)
negative reinforcement	manipulation
positive punishment	shaped
negative punishment	target
positively reinforce (ed)	baseline
negatively reinforce (ed)	strength (en)
positively punish (ed)	satisfaction
negatively punish (ed)	competing behavior
generalize (ed)	discrimination
consistent (ly)	mixed messages
increasing	secondary
decreasing	pinpoint

operationally
positive reinforcer (s)
punishment
antecedent (s)
positively reinforcing
extinguish (ed)
extinction
classical conditioning
operant conditioning
neutral stimulus
discriminative stimulus
operantly
rate
maladaptive
extinguish (ed)
appropriate (ly)
inappropriate (ly)
contingent
noncontingently
social reinforcer

social reinforcement
consequence (s)
attention
strengthened (ed)
strengthening
weaken (ed)
weakening
ignored
shaping
continuous
intermittent
tangible
social
primary
attend
intermittently reinforcing
shape (d)
frequency
latency
duration

Case One

A cute, four-year-old boy's father would come home every night, drink a few beers, eat, watch T.V., and go to sleep, not attending to the boy. The boy was becoming more withdrawn in front of other people, and more of a problem at home. He had no physical illness or problem, but would tantrum, shout, cry and throw things. The father would then either hit him or shake him or tousle his hair and call him "his little tiger." Soon, the mother had to bring the child into a clinic for help in controlling the boy.

In this short story we can see that the father was a very potent _________________________ for his son. When the father did not attend to his little boy he was in essence _____________________ withdrawing his attention. Any good behavior exhibited was ignored and therefore became _____________________; however, if he began to behave _____________________ (i.e. shout, throw things) he would make his father attend to him. The little boy misbehaved so that as a ________________ his father would ________________ to him; in other words he was being ________________ for having tantrums. The father would hit his son for having tantrums, but sometimes he would call him his little tiger; therefore ________________ the behavior which could only serve to ________________ it. In other words the father has managed to create a situation where giving his attention to his little boy is ________________ upon the latter exhibiting ________________ behaviors. Any intervention program would have to focus upon ________________ the inappropriate behavior and re-establishing the appropriate behaviors. In this particular case ________________ and ________________ must be changed. Tantrums should be ________________ which means removing the ________ ________________ which was ________________ ________ ________________. In other words tantrums should be ________ ________ ________________. At the same time all instances of good behavior however small should receive a lot of ________________ therefore gradually ________________ the little boy to interact appropriately.

Case Two

Joey is an autistic boy of five. When he hears his mother telling him "Joey, it is time to go to bed," he starts to tantrum (i.e. running up and down the hall screaming and biting anyone who tries to forcefully put him to bed). The same thing has happened for the past two months every night with its getting worse and worse. On each successive tantrum the mother has tried to ignore Joey, but he would only tantrum louder and longer to the point where she was forced to intervene (tell him he didn't have to go to bed yet). At this point Joey was allowed to stay up as long as he wanted. Any attempt to make him go to bed resulted in an all-night tantrum.

The mother telling him to go to bed could be the ________________ for Joey to tantrum. Initially, telling him to go to bed was a ________________ ________________. The tantrum behavior could have become ________________ conditioned when

its consequence led to _______________ or rather the removal
or termination of the _______________ of going to bed. The
mother's attention to Joey's tantrum acted as a _______________
_______________ further _______________ the tantrum.
The process whereby mother gave in to Joey for longer and louder tantrums is called _______________ a response. The tantrum has been under a _______________ schedule of reinforcement. The goal of the intervention program is to _______________
the behavior of having tantrums by making the tantrum _______
_______________ upon either the removal of the _______________
_______________ or the institution of an _______________
_______________. or both. Doing either of these is called
_______________. While inappropriate behaviors are _______
_______________ the appropriate behaviors of not having tantrums
and going to bed quietly will receive reinforcement and therefore
be _______________.

Case Three

John and Joan have been married for thirty years. Over the
years friends have noticed some idiosyncracies of the couple. Occasionally, whenever John didn't want to talk about an issue (because he said it was very distressing) he would do one of three
things: (1) he would walk away, (2) sometimes declare his position to be correct without citing reasons, or (3) attack the other
person (s) over an issue totally superfluous and irrelevant to the
discussion. When John did any one of these things in the beginning of their marriage, Joan's initial reaction was to apologize for
John's behavior. Over the years Joan eventually began to sense
circumstances which would lead to John's behavior. As she became proficient at this, she prevented the possibility of an explo-
sive situation by using a series of tactics. First she would explain
John's position on an issue, knowing full well that John would
not. Second, she would elaborate upon what she thought was
John's viewpoint in an attempt to make it look more credible.
Finally, if people were still insistent in pressing John for an
answer, she would simply tell people to "Drop it, don't you know
this is not the right time; you force him into a corner; he doesn't

mean to be like that; you have to give him time to think; and later, when he is calm, I will talk to him and I am sure I can make him listen." These tactics employed by Joan were usually used in front of John and were used by Joan with increasing if not startling success over the years. People having grievances with John or who were in need of advice would instead go to Joan who would then communicate to John (who would be sitting in the same room with the parties concerned). This "interpretation" was justified as necessary because "John's problem was that he sometimes didn't understand what you were saying." Once interpreted John would either address his remarks to the person or to Joan with the additional remark "You're the one that asked me the question, aren't you?"

John's tactics for avoiding a conversation are the _______________ _______________ he exhibits in those situations. The fact that his behavior increased over the years indicated that they were _______ _______________ _______________ by the removal of the aversive situation and _______________ _______________ by his learning that Joan would "do it for him" when those situations arose. Thus John's increase in the behavior meant that it was _______________ and, as well, it _______________ to more situations which were less aversive yet still received adequate _______________. Joan's ability to predict circumstances leading to John's behavior is a good example of how, in a nonsystematic fashion, we all employ the identification technique in order to determine _______________ and _______________. In this situation Joan became more adept at manipulating the _______________. It is important to remember that Joan's becoming more adept at the prediction of the possible situation and her successful _______________ of the situation, served as a _______________ _______________ which removed the possibly aversive behavior of John. Thus, Joan's ability just described was similar to the process called _______________. The behavior of the other people was also _______________.

Before using any intervention techniques it is important to _______________, or target the inappropriate behaviors which means that we must _______________ define them. Next it is important to obtain some _________________ measure of the behavior's strength. This can be done by recording any one or combination of the following: Do a _________________ count, _________________ measure, measure the behavior's _________ _________ or obtain the behavior _________________. Next we must identify the _________________ and _________________ of the behavior. After this we must establish a program which must be carried out consistently. The main emphasis should be placed upon _________________ adaptive behaviors while concomitantly _________________maladaptive behaviors. In this example the wrong technique would be to tell John he is wrong, or _________ _________ _________________ John contingently upon his exhibiting the behavior. This is because the _________________ is precisely what John wanted to avoid; therefore, employing such a tactic which initially caused his _________________ behavior can not now _________________ adaptive behavior. It would probably be a better approach if we _________________ _________________ any appropriate conversational behavior John exhibits while at the same time letting his maladaptive behavior (the three tactics) lead to some neutral consequence (i.e. Joan does not intercede and everyone ignores John when he acts inappropriately) thereby _________________ his tactics concomitantly with _________________ conversational behavior.

Case Four

A schizophrenic patient (P) who confuses "yes" with "no." The psychiatrist is interested in his abnormal behavior as a sign of his supposed internal conflicts. When *P* said normal things, he was ignored, when he said abnormal things, the psychiatrist would perk up and ask him why he said it, did he really mean it, or did he mean the opposite. The psychiatrist would also ask the *P* if he wanted a cigarette. When the *P* said "No!" he was given it anyway and he smoked it while the psychiatrist probed with further questions. The psychiatrist pointed out that the *P* was saying "No" more often, even to food and that he was becoming more confused.*

---

*Staats, A.: Learning theory and opposite speech. *J Abnorm Psychol, 55*:268-69, 1957.

The act of ignoring the patient when he said appropriate things is explained in terms of _______________ withdrawal of attention which is the _______________ _______________. This is also called _______________ _______________ and will result in _______________ the appropriate conversations of the patient. However, every time the patient says something abnormal the psychiatrist "perks up" and gives the patient a lot of attention, therefore _______________ _______________ him on a _______________ reinforcement schedule. When the patient was asked the question "Do you want a cigarette?", saying "No" made the experimenter give it to him. He was therefore again being _______________ _______________ with the cigarette a _______________ reinforcer and attention which is a _______________ _______________ reinforcer. As the experimenter reported and as we would expect to happen the reversal of "No" for "Yes" was _______________. The patient would even say "No" to food which is a _______________ reinforcer showing that he had _______________ the reversal of yes and no. The best way to weaken the inappropriate behavior would be to withhold the attention and the cigarette (or food) which were potent _______________ _______________ for the patient's abnormal speech. In other words _______________ _______________ him.

Concomitantly all appropriate speech should receive a lot of _______________ _______________. It is important that the program be carried out _______________ for if the patient is sometimes positively reinforced for reversing "No" and "Yes" or talking inappropriately he will be on an _______________ schedule of reinforcement and his behavior will be _______________ instead of _______________.

ANSWERS TO QUESTIONS

Classical versus Operant Conditioning

1. a	7. c	13. false
2. c	8. c	14. false
3. c	9. b	15. false
4. b	10. false	16. true
5. e	11. true	17. true
6. d	12. false	

Measurement

1. d (a and b)	7. c
2. a	8. c
3. c	9. e
4. d	10. true
5. e	11. false
6. a	12. false

Types of Reinforcement

1. e	8. c
2. a	9. b
3. d	10. true
4. f	11. true
5. c	12. true
6. d (b and c)	13. true
7. a	14. true

Reinforcement Effect

1. e	7. e
2. b	8. false
3. e (a, c and d)	9. false
4. d	10. true
5. b	11. false
6. d	12. false

Schedules of Reinforcement

1. b	7. true
2. b	8. false
3. d	9. false
4. b	10. true
5. d	11. false
6. true	

Shaping and Ways to Decrease Maladaptive Behavior

1. e	7. a	13. d	19. false
2. b	8. a	14. false	20. true
3. e	9. a	15. true	
4. e	10. a	16. true	
5. b	11. a	17. true	
6. b	12. a	18. false	

Answers to Case Fill-in-The-Blanks
(answers are in the order that they appear in the cases)

One
social reinforcer
noncontingently
extinguished
inappropriately
consequence
attend
positively reinforced
intermittently reinforcing
strengthen
contingent
inappropriate
weakening
antecedents
consequences
ignored
attention
positive reinforcer
negatively punished
attention
shaping

Two
discriminative stimulus
neutral stimulus
operantly
negative reinforcement
aversive stimulus
positive reinforcer
strengthening
shaping
continuous
weaken
contingent
positive reinforcement

aversive stimulus
punishment
weakened
strengthened

Three
behaviors
negatively reinforced
positively reinforced
strengthened
generalized
reinforcement
antecedents
consequences
antecedents
manipulation
negative reinforcement
shaping
shaped
pinpoint
operationally
baseline
frequency
latency
duration
rate
antecedents
consequences
strengthening
weakening
positively punish
positive punishment
maladaptive
strengthen
positively reinforced

(answers to cases continued)
weakening
strengthening

Four
contingent
positive reinforcement
negative punishment
weakening
positively reinforcing
continuous
positively reinforced
tangible

social
strengthened
primary
generalized
positive reinforcers
negatively punish
positive reinforcement
consistently
intermittent
increasing
decreasing

APPENDIX IV

GLOSSARY OF BEHAVIORAL TERMS

accelerating — an increase in the rate of a behavior

activity reinforcers — a preferred activity; one which the child already does frequently and seems to enjoy that can be used to reinforce a less preferred activity or behavior, e.g. staying up late, playing with a toy, eating dessert, watching TV

adaptive behavior — appropriate behavior; behavior that is soundly acceptable

antecedent — what happens before a behavior occurs

appropriate behaviors — socially acceptable behaviors; "good" behaviors that you wish to strengthen, adaptive behaviors

aversive — something "bad" or unpleasant; consequences which usually hurt; an undesirable stimulus

avoid — to stay away from

axis — a straight line for measurement on a graph

baseline — data collected before any program or intervention begins; the strength of the behavior before change

behavioral contracting — involves writing down and agreeing upon specific behaviors and the contingencies to be used in changing behavior

behavior repertoire — the full range of behaviors that a child exhibits

competing response — behaviors that you try to substitute in place of maladaptive behaviors; by strengthening the competing response you hope to weaken the target behavior; incompatible behavior

components	the parts that make up the whole behavior
consequence	events which occur following behaviors which can strengthen or weaken such behaviors; reinforcers and punishers are consequences
contingent	according to a rule; depending on something that has occurred; whether or not a reinforcer is given is *contingent* upon (depends upon) when the response occurs
criticism trap	the parent is reinforced for scolding or hurting by the child's stopping his misbehavior for a while; parent is trapped by being negatively reinforced for scolding, which increases in strength until it is the only means of control used
deceleration	slowing of the rate, decrease of strength of a behavior as shown on a decreasing curve on a graph
delay of reinforcement	time occurs between the behavior and the reinforcer
discriminate	responding differently in different situations; established when behavior is reinforced in one situation and not in another
elicit	to draw forth a behavior (e.g. an infant's crying elicits concern in the mother)
encopresis	incontinent for fecal elimination
enuretic	incontinent, not toilet trained for urination
escape	to get away from
explicit	directly stated, made clear
extinction	removing all reinforcement as a means of weakening behavior
extrinsic motivation	performing for reinforcers diagnosed by someone else
frequency	the number of times a behavior occurs

generalizing	the occurrence of a response in situations other than the situations in which it was reinforced
identification	observing a behavior and its consequences and antecedents
inappropriate behaviors	socially unacceptable behaviors; "bad" behaviors that you wish to weaken; maladaptive behaviors
inhibit	stopping a behavior from continuing
interventions	programs whereby the strength of a behavior is changed by controlling antecedents or consequences
intermittent	occurring now and then, not every time; a behavior intermittently reinforced is not reinforced every single time it occurs
intrinsic motivation	performing for no tangible reinforcers but for "self-pride" or "satisfaction"
magnitude	the strength of a response
manipulation	controlling antecedents or consequences to change the strength of a behavior
mixed messages	rules and demands made upon the child that are unclear and contradictory (e.g. father says one thing; mother another)
model	something to be imitated or patterned upon (e.g. boys model their father)
motivator	drive; something that causes the child to do something
negative reinforcer	something aversive that is removed following a behavior that is to be strengthened
noncontingent	a reinforcer that comes whether or not a specific behavior is emitted, not dependent on rules or whether something else has occurred
pinpoint	to target; to describe the problem in terms of the behaviors exhibited

positive reinforcer — a reward, something desired or pleasant that is presented after a behavior to be strengthened

primary reinforcer — unlearned reinforcers; do not have to be paired with any other reinforcer to be effective in strengthening behavior they follow (e.g. food, water)

program — a planned intervention for systematically changing behavior

punishment — the weakening of a behavior through the presentation of aversive consequences, or the withdrawal of reinforcing consequences

rate — the number of times a behavior occurs per unit of time; computed by dividing the frequency of behavior by the amount of time observing

reinforcement — to strengthen a behavior through the presentation of positive consequences or the removal of negative consequences

reversal — a return to the conditions preceding the institution of a program; return to baseline conditions

secondary reinforcement — learned reinforcer; reinforcer that gets its power through being paired with an already effective reinforcer (e.g. mother's smile; verbal praise; tokens)

self-stimulatory — repetitive, usually stereotyped behaviors that are probably reinforced by their own performance, seen often in autistic children (e.g. hand flapping; rocking, head-banging)

shaping — reinforcing closer and closer approximations of the desired behavior

significant — greater than a chance occurrence

social reinforcers — reinforcers found in the behavior of other people (e.g. smiling, winking, saying "good," "I love you," a pat on the arm)

strengthen	to increase the rate at which a behavior occurs
suppress	to weaken a behavior's strength
systematic analysis	an orderly objective study of a problem
tangible or material reinforcers	objects or anything material that can be given to the child as a reinforcer (e.g. candy, a doll, a new dress)
target behavior	the behaviors selected to be strengthened or weakened through a program
time out	the removal of positive reinforcers following behavior to be weakened; usually involves placing a child alone in a room, away from all sound reinforcers for a short period.
warning signal	a learned punisher, a signal which has been closely followed by a punisher and which *indicates* punishment might be coming
weaken	to decrease the rate at which a behavior occurs
weaning	movement from extrinsic to intrinsic reinforcers; less dependence on reinforcers administered by someone else and greater dependence upon one's own internal reinforcers (e.g. satisfaction, competency)

SUBJECT INDEX